The Sierra Club Totebooks®

The Best About Backpacking
Bitterroot to Beartooth
The Climber's Guide to the High Sierra
Climber's Guide to Yosemite Valley
Climbing and Hiking in the Wind River Mountains
Cooking for Camp and Trail
Fieldbook of Nature Photography
Food for Knapsackers
Footloose in the Swiss Alps
Hiker's Guide to the Smokies
Hiking the Bigfoot Country
Hiking the Grand Canyon
Hiking the Great Basin
Hiking the North Cascades
Hiking the Old Dominion
Hiking the Southwest
Hiking the Teton Backcountry
Hiking the Yellowstone Backcountry
Hut Hopping in the Austrian Alps
Starr's Guide to the John Muir Trail and the High
  Sierra Region
Timberline Country
To Walk With a Quiet Mind
Words for the Wild

A Sierra Club Totebook®

Cooking for Camp and Trail

by Hasse Bunnelle
with Shirley Sarvis

Sierra Club Books   •   San Francisco

The Sierra Club, founded in 1892 by John Muir, has devoted itself to the study and protection of the earth's scenic and ecological resources—mountains, wetlands, woodlands, wild shores and rivers, deserts and plains. The publishing program of the Sierra Club offers books to the public as a nonprofit educational service in the hope that they may enlarge the public's understanding of the Club's basic concerns. The point of view expressed in each book, however, does not necessarily represent that of the Club. The Sierra Club has some sixty chapters coast to coast, in Canada, Hawaii, and Alaska. For information about how you may participate in its program to preserve wilderness and the quality of life, please address inquiries to Sierra Club, 730 Polk Street, San Francisco, CA 94109.

Library of Congress Catalog Card Number 77-189535.
International Standard Book Number 87156-006-6.

Designed by Charles Curtis, Inc. New York, and printed in the United States of America.

10   9   8   7

Introduction

Some years ago I was camped one miserably cold rainy evening by the Big Bend of the Columbia River in British Columbia. My job was preparing the soup, and it proved to be a challenge, because every time I removed the lid to stir the mixture, a wave of gigantic mosquitoes dive-bombed down the steam column into the cook pot.

One summer a few years earlier I drove west after college with friends in a poor beat-up station wagon. We were *all* poor, in fact, because babysitting and odd jobs hadn't provided enough for car repair or decent meals. To climb a difficult Black Hill we had to back the wagon up again and again, until we made it on the third try; we lived for five days on a certain brand of Irish stew, heated in the can.

When my financial status had improved considerably, I went car camping on the south coast of Turkey. Owing to the fact that my group had planned to eat all its meals at "little colorful local restaurants," and we never found *any* restaurants, we made do for four days on the snacks we'd taken along to go with the drinks. Survivors of the expedition refer to it as "our four-day cocktail party."

Well, now, you campers. If you want to look canned stew in the face again, but you don't look forward to four days' worth of Vienna sausage, and you choose to get your protein from sources other than suicidal mosquitoes, you will make good use of this book. Here are some 200 new recipes — intended not only for backpackers but also, as Hasse Bunnelle says, for those traveling "by car, raft, rowboat, pack animal and dog sled." Recipes as well for all those "camper" campers to whom weight and space are not critical considerations. Dishes so toothsome that you may decide to whip them up for a backyard feast, without going anywhere at all.

Cooking for Camp and Trail picks up where our earlier Totebook, *Food for Knapsackers and Other Trail Travelers*, leaves off. In *Knapsackers* weight was the primary consideration. And the emphasis, in one sense, was on the back. The emphasis here is on the stomach. If you own *Knapsackers*, though, you may recognize some old friends here, such as Golden (Bob) Trout Parmesan. That and a few others were judged to be just too ideally mouth-watering to leave out, and are repeated for the benefit of campers who don't have access to the first book. Still, if you're backpacking and feeding groups of five or twenty, we recommend your investing in a copy of *Food for Knapsackers*. The two books complement each other.

They also share the same author — Hasse Bunnelle. Hasse, a lifelong outdoor enthusiast, was born in the South Dakota Badlands country and grew up on the Plains of west Texas. She had an early interest in cooking, particularly in the seasoning of food. Since joining the Sierra Club in 1953, she has cooked for about two

8

dozen club wilderness outings, and innumerable week-end trips. She is an editor for the Federation of Western Outdoor Clubs, and for the Sierra Club *Wildlife News-letter*.

Food writer Shirley Sarvis edited Hasse's collection of recipes. She has written five cookbooks of her own. West Coast readers may be familiar with her *San Francisco Firehouse Favorites*. Additionally, her magazine articles appear in *Gourmet, Better Homes and Gardens, Sunset,* and *Woman's Day*. Shirley lives in San Francisco where she also free-lances as a consultant on food and wine. The Sierra Club is proud to be in print with a writer of such "great integrity," to quote *The New York Times*.

Campers' meals can range from the Spartan to the exotic. But we believe that even the Spartan should be tasty; this book therefore includes suggestions for the full range. Just have a look: Granola. Sourdough Pancakes. Wine-Marinated Steak. Glazed Carrots and Apples. Rabbit *Borracho*.

So pack up, slip the Tote in your pocket, and be on your way. And don't blame us if the cake falls!

— *Constance L. Stallings*

Acknowledgments

When John Mitchell, editor-in-chief of Sierra Club Books, asked me whether I could round up 200 recipes for camp and trail, I said yes, because I knew I had more than a hundred suitable recipes of my own. Then, during the summer of 1971, I phoned all the outdoor cooks I could think of. I found very few at home; most were on the trail or river, as is proper for outings people. Nevertheless, I had some success:

For recipes I am grateful to Linda Benamati, Emily Benner, Dina Bloomer, Wes Bunnelle, Anne Chamberlain, Paul Friedman, Roxanne Friedman, Bob Golden, Ketty Johnson, Adina and Gordon Robinson, Mary Townsend, and Bob Wenkam. I thank Bob Braun, Ted Grubb and Tom Pillsbury for technical information about stoves and fuel, and Anne Brower for general encouragement. Also the members of the fall 1971 Dark Canyon Outing, on whom recipes were tested, and the hundreds of campers on other Sierra Club outings who have shared my successful dishes and disasters, in all kinds of weather.

I hope Shirley Sarvis found in my recipes more order than is usually reflected by my cooking habits. Much of my pleasure in camp cooking lies in finding new combinations of food to try over the cook fire.

I hope other camp cooks will experiment, too.

— *Hasse Bunnelle*
San Francisco

Contents

INTRODUCTION   7

ACKNOWLEDGMENTS 10

PREPARATION
Planning and Food Purchasing 13
Basic Calculations 20
Timing and Temperature Variables 21
Glossary of Cooking Terms 22

RECIPES
Breakfasts and Trail Snacks 24
Lunch Suggestions 30
Soups 32
Meats, Poultry, Fish 37
Eggs and Cheese 103
Potatoes, Rice, Dry Beans, Grains 110
Vegetables 119
Salads 125
Breads and Pancakes 143

Sauces, Condiments, Dressings 152
Desserts 158
Beverages 169

APPENDIX
Packaging the Food 174
Tips for Backpackers 176
Cooking Equipment Lists 177
Stoves, Ovens, and Bags 180
Building a Fire 183
Washing Dishes 184
Storing Food 185
Breaking Camp 186
The Camping Ethic 187

SOME SUPPLIERS OF LIGHTWEIGHT FOOD . . . 188

INDEX OF RECIPES 191

12

Preparation

Planning and Food Purchasing

The type and length of your camping trip will determine your menus. The requirements of a backpack trip, with emphasis on lightweight, low-bulk items, differ from those of a camper trip on which weight and bulk are important (but not major) considerations, and refrigeration provides storage for some fresh meat and vegetables. But no matter what kind of trip you are taking, a carefully chosen mixture of freeze-dried, dehydrated, canned, and fresh foods will provide a nutritious and varied diet. And remember, it's *always* bright to travel light.

Active people require a high protein diet. Protein and fat digest slowly, and should be present in all meals. A breakfast including a protein and some fat will alleviate the hunger that comes all too soon after a breakfast of only carbohydrates, or only fruit and cereal. Keep down the sugar and starch content of your meals. Such foods are filling but not satisfying, and while a little candy is useful for quick energy snacks, protein foods provide a higher level of energy.

Carefully planned diets contain sufficient quantities of vitamins and minerals for most people but because cooking destroys Vitamin C, supplements of that are advisable for any trip more than a few days long. If there is any question about the nutritional content of your canned or dried foods, add vitamin and mineral supplements. Take whole-grained cereals, fresh meats, nuts, vegetables, and few if any highly refined foods.

Organic or Natural Foods. All foods are organic, but as usually used today the word describes those foods grown without pesticides or chemical fertilizers, canned without chemical additives, and prepared for the market without excessive refining.

There are not many naturally grown fresh fruits and vegetables on the market: health food stores, cooperative markets, and farmers' markets are the best outlets. Yet mountaineering shops and supermarkets are responding to the increasing campers' demand for better foods in dried, packaged form. You should check carefully the quality, price and source of each item, and comparative prices per pound.

Backpackers, hikers, climbers, canoeists and skiiers need high calorie, high protein diets — more so than provided by most of the "organic vegetarian" diets currently popular, especially with young people. If you are into a vegetarian diet, be sure it contains at least 65 grams of high quality protein for every 3,000 calories — the number of calories an active sportsman probably needs. Soy is an excellent source of vegetable protein; and soy flour can be used in many ways. Other beans, peas, lentils and brown rice are good but less complete sources, and therefore should not be relied upon (entirely). Milk, eggs, and cheese contain high quality protein and should be included in any vegetarian diet. The hard cheeses keep particularly well and being light in weight, are excellent for camping.

All beans, peas, and lentils can be used to replace potatoes and rice (ounce for ounce, dehydrated weight) in soup or stew. For additional flavor and nutrition, add 1 to 2 tablespoons of wheat germ or brewers yeast per serving to the cooking pot.

Vegetarian campers will find that many of the recipes in this book, especially in the sections on eggs, vegetables, and salads, are appropriate for their diets.

Menu Planning. For efficient menu planning, you should draw a chart. Establish columns of meals across the top of a page of paper: dinner (first, for ease in keeping track of "camp days"), breakfast, lunch, snacks, and a column for staples and miscellaneous items such as soap, cleaning equipment, and gloves. Down the side of the page, write the days and dates of your trip. Then fill in for each meal of each day the exact amount of every item required — whether a fruit or meat, ingredient in soup, stew or dessert. Lastly on a separate page list all the items, and total the amounts. This will serve as your shopping list for the trip.

Don't forget to list all seasonings you plan to use, plus a few more you might decide to use en route. Herbs and spices add very little weight or bulk, and are immensely valuable in bringing camp cooking as close to gourmet standards as possible. So don't stint on them. Salt can be figured generously, but be more stingy with sugar. Include a few extra bouillon cubes, some extra chocolate, tea and coffee — for safety if you are going into the back country, or to feed unexpected guests. There should be no less than 1¼ pounds of food per person per day. Never plan too closely, even on trips where lightness is vital.

Purchasing Notes. You can improve your menus by adding a touch of color to one meal and something salty to another. When you shop, be on the lookout for new items. Herbs serve well, as do spices and a grating of lemon rind over soup or dessert. Horehound or peppermint sticks dress up a cup of tea, or can be eaten on the trail. A dollop of caviar in an omelet weighs little and is not too costly to add once. Nowadays you can buy anchovies in paste form, in tubes; pack a tube to add to salads, omelets, or crackers at the social hour. You will find that fresh air and new surroundings stimulate your senses and enhance your enjoyment of fragrances and flavors.

Cheese. Buy only good hard cheeses — never the sliced processed kind. Without refrigeration, the latter melt quickly and then start molding. Anyway, they lack the flavor and body of hard cheeses.

For a 2- or 3-day hike, buy each member of your group an individual Edam cheese for lunch. Leave the wax coating on them. A 1-pound Longhorn is just right for camping. Or buy cheese in wedges cut from wheels, or slabs cut from blocks. You can seal the cut sides for traveling by covering them with cheesecloth, and dipping them into hot paraffin.

Some other good cheeses: sharp or mild cheddar, Swiss, Monterey Jack, Tybo, Norbo. Port Salut is a fine dessert cheese. Sapsago (hard goat cheese) is excellent when grated into breakfast eggs and omelets, stews, and soups. It keeps almost forever; if it gets too hard, you can soak it in a little water to resoften it for grating. (Save the soaking water to add to your next stew or soup.)

Lunch Meats. Hard salamis, smoked meats, and jerky are readily available in individual and larger packages, and are excellent foods to take along on camping trips.

Meats. If fresh meats are appropriate for your trip, consider taking 1- to 2-inch thick chuck roasts for broiling as steaks. To serve, slice diagonally like London broil. A better cut of meat with more flavor and less fat is a boneless cross-rib roast; broil it, also. These cuts are less expensive than standard cuts of steak, and contain less fat.

Do not neglect organ, or variety, meats. Pound for pound they provide more nutrition than red meats, and prepared properly they are delicious. Whenever possible, use liver, heart, tongue (smoked tongue is good), brains, and tripe. But be sure the meat is fresh and odorless, and cook it at once. Chicken livers on a skewer are a welcome change from canned or dried meats. Do *not* cook liver so long it becomes hard and dry; sauté it until it is just past the pink stage. (Onions and bacon are good but not necessary accompaniments.) Overcooking meat destroys food value and flavor. Any "well-done" meat should be cooked just enough to eliminate the pink color, but no more, to avoid loss of nutrients and flavorful juices, and toughening of the fibers.

Fish. Except for smoked or canned varieties, fish don't travel well. Buy smoked fish in preference to canned: smoked fish can be used in a variety of ways for all meals. The smoky, salty flavors blend well with camp surroundings. Old-fashioned salted codfish in a 1-pound

17

box is an excellent buy. In camp, soak and wash it well, and make into a stew (see Lamarou on page 100) or flake and mix with equal amounts of mashed potato, a bit of parsley, and pepper, form into cakes, and sauté for breakfast or dinner. Fish helps fill the "protein for breakfast" requirement on lightweight trips.

Vegetables. Use vegetables — dried, frozen, canned, or fresh — whenever, wherever, possible, for flavor, nutrition, and color. Avoid the Potato-Only or Rice-Only route. Experiment with bulghour wheat, dried beans, black-eyed peas, and lentils. All are high in protein. Plan on dried foods expanding about three times when cooked. As for weight: freeze-dried meats and vegetables are lighter than dried foods but occupy about the same volume as the food when fresh. Food packages and some supply catalogues list dry weight and cooked weights, and changes in bulk. A few freeze-dried and dehydrated measurements are included in Basic Calculations, page 19.

Fruits. Whenever possible, take fresh fruit. An orange in the lunch sack the first day or two will be welcome. Additionally, there are many freeze-dried fruits that, if bulky, are lightweight and reconstitute well. Regular dried fruits are good for breakfast, lunch, and trail snacks. If weight is no problem, a few canned fruits can be refreshing for breakfast and quick desserts. But most brands carry extra weight in sugar syrup, so you should watch the proportion of syrup to fruit when choosing your purchase.

Nuts. Always take nuts. There may be bulk suppliers in your neighborhood from whom you can buy broken nuts for less than the whole ones on your supermarket shelves.

Candy. Hard candies, paper wrapped, are the best type of candy for camp and trail. Chocolate candy is popular in cold weather but doesn't keep its shape in the summer. Squares of cooking chocolate behave better.

Beverages. Many freeze-dried beverages are available in the stores; they are ideal for all kinds of camping. Fruit crystal drinks are preferable to imitation fruit-flavored ones. Most stores now stock a wide variety of tea bags.

Staples. Pack only as much flour (or meal) as you plan to use in your recipes. It is heavy stuff. Buy enough milk to cover cooking needs, cereals and beverages. Nutritionists recommend 1 pint of milk per day per adult. You can estimate consumption of sugar at 1 ounce per person per day, or 1½ ounces for younger people, especially those in their teens.

The Condiment Cache. Fresh foods carry such rich and varied flavors that you can enjoy most of them without seasonings. But most canned foods, all freeze-dried meats, and most freeze-dried vegetables need some additional seasoning to make them palatable.

A cook's use of herbs, chili peppers, seeds, a curry blend, and sweet spices can add a great deal of zest to a camping menu. Dried herbs are the most available and most convenient for camp cooks' use, although fresh ones are invariably preferable for taste.

Small markets near resorts, parks, and other camping areas seldom offer much variety in seasonings. So gather a selection of seasonings before you leave on your trip, pack them in small labeled containers (35mm film cans are excellent), put them into a plastic bag or box, and keep them within easy reach when cooking.

Here is a suggested list of the most useful condiments to take along with you:

Salt
Garlic cloves
Celery salt
Cayenne
Crushed dried
    hot red peppers
Anise and/or fennel seed
Dried oregano leaves
Dried basil leaves
Dried dill weed
Ground cloves
Vanilla extract

Ground black pepper
Garlic powder
Tabasco sauce
Chili powder
Curry powder
Sesame seed
Dried tarragon leaves
Dried marjoram leaves
Ground cinnamon
Ground nutmeg
Lemon extract

Basic Calculations

Measurements
    3 teaspoons = 1 tablespoon
    16 tablespoons = 1 cup
    2 cups = 1 pint
    2 pints = 1 quart
    4 quarts = 1 gallon
    16 ounces = 1 pound
    Sierra Club cup = 10 ounces or 1¼ measuring cups

Milk from powdered milk
    4 ounces milk powder plus 1 quart water = 1 quart milk
    1 pound milk powder plus 1 gallon water = 1 gallon milk

**Typical per-person, per-serving weights for
some freeze-dried and dehydrated foods**

Green beans (freeze-dried)	.25 ounces
Cabbage dices (freeze-dried)	.4 to .5 ounces
Carrot dices (freeze-dried)	.4 to .5 ounces
Corn (freeze-dried)	.5 to .6 ounces
Peas (freeze-dried)	.5 to .6 ounces

Potato dices (dehydrated)	1.2 to 1.5 ounces
Potato flour	
or flakes (instant)	1.5 to 1.8 ounces
Spinach flakes (dehydrated)	.4 to .5 ounces
Tomato flakes (dehydrated)	.4 to .5 ounces
Yam or sweet	
potato flakes (dehydrated)	1.5 to 1.8 ounces

Timing and Temperature Variables

Timings and temperatures in camp cookery cannot be precise because campfires, equipment, altitudes, ingredients, and cooks vary. So consider the timings and temperatures in the following recipes as general guides — approximations to use as references — rather than precision finalities. In camp cooking, that long-scorned cook's maxim, "cook until done," is really the right measure.

The temperatures and timings of the recipes are for cooking at sea level. As your camp altitude increases, you will need to increase your cooking time accordingly.

Some general guidelines for high-altitude cooking.

—For food that cooks at sea level in less than 20 minutes: Add 1 minute cooking time for each 1,000 feet above sea level.

—For food that takes more than 20 minutes to cook at sea level: Add 2 minutes cooking time for each 1,000 feet above sea level.

—For freeze-dried and dehydrated foods: Most require little cooking after the soaking period, so usually no extra time is necessary.

—For soups, stews, and other simmered camp foods: Whatever the altitude, add water or some other liquid as necessary to prevent burning and to keep the dish at the proper consistency.

21

Altitude variables to keep in mind while baking.

—Because air pressure decreases as altitude increases, batter requires less beating to lighten it at high altitudes than at sea level.

—Because thermometer temperatures are actually higher at upper elevations than at lower ones, sugar and shortening burn relatively faster. And breads and cakes will rise — and fall — relatively faster at high elevations. So at higher elevations, lower the baking heat. Additionally, make the following recipe changes.

Above 5,000 feet: Reduce each 1 teaspoon of baking powder by ¼ teaspoon

Reduce each 1 cup sugar by 2 tablespoons

Increase each 1 cup liquid by 2 to 3 tablespoons

Above 7,000 feet: Reduce each 1 teaspoon of baking powder by ¼ teaspoon

Reduce each 1 cup sugar by 2 to 3 tablespoons

Increase each 1 cup liquid by 3 to 4 tablespoons

At elevations much higher than 7,000 feet, the variables in baking increase, and become more complicated. If you plan to do a good deal of high-altitude baking, you should make a more specialized study of the subject than this book allows.

Glossary of Cooking Terms

Boiling — Cooking in water at a temperature of 212° Fahrenheit at sea level. The water bubbles vigorously and gives off steam. (Boiling temperature lowers as altitude increases.)

Parboiling — Boiling food briefly before preparing in other ways. It takes the fight out of tough foods.

Poaching — Cooking eggs or fish for a short time in liquids just below the boiling point.

Simmering — Cooking in water at a temperature of 180° F. to 210° F. at sea level — or just below the boiling point.

Stewing — Simmering in a small amount of water or other liquid.

Steaming — Cooking in steam.

Braising — Browning in shortening, then simmering, covered.

Broiling — Cooking over or under direct heat such as camp fires, hot coals, gas flame, or electric unit.

Pan-broiling — Cooking on a lightly oiled hot griddle or heavy pan.

Deep-frying — Cooking food in deep fat heated to about 350° F. to 400° F. at sea level.

Sautéing — Cooking or browning in very little shortening.

Roasting — Cooking before an open fire or in an open pan in an oven (dry heat).

Baking — Cooking in an oven (dry heat).

Recipes

Breakfasts and Trail Snacks

Instant Breakfast   **1 serving**

This is a good quick breakfast before an early hike. The fruit ingredient may be whatever fresh fruits are in season, such as peaches, bananas, apricots, berries, pears. Or it may be poached and chilled dried fruits such as apricots, prunes, pears, apples, peaches, or a mixture of several.

4 ounces wheat germ
1 cup sliced fresh fruit or 1 cup poached dried fruit
½ cup milk
1 tablespoon honey

Stir all ingredients together.

24

Quick Trail Breakfast   1 serving

4 ounces granola-type cereal (Vita Grains and Nuts)
2 to 4 ounces powdered milk
Raisins to taste
Honey (optional)
Cold or boiling water

Stir together milk, cereal, raisins, and honey. Add water according to taste.

Buckwheat Groats (for Breakfast)   4 servings

1 pound groats
Water
Honey
Milk

Heat and stir groats in a heavy frying pan until they are toasted. Add enough water just to cover groats. Heat to boiling. Remove from heat, cover, and let stand for 10 minutes or until the grain absorbs the water. Serve with honey and milk.

Dried Apples

Dry the apples at home, package in plastic bags, and take to camp for tasty snacks along the trail.

12 apples, peeled, quartered, and cored

Very thinly slice apples using the thin-slicing side of a food grater. Spread in a shallow layer on a lightly greased baking sheet, and bake in a very slow oven (250°) until dry, about 20 to 30 minutes. Turn once during baking.

Granola **About 4½ quarts**

Eat as is for lunch or trail snacks. Or add hot or cold water according to taste.

½ to 1 cup wheat germ
1 cup powdered milk
1 cup shredded or grated coconut
¼ to ½ cup vegetable oil
4 to 5 cups regular oatmeal or other grain
3 cups chopped walnuts or other nuts
2 cups mixed sesame seeds and shelled sunflower seeds
5 cups mixed dried fruits (peaches, pears, apples, raisins, figs, apricots), finely chopped
½ cup honey
¼ cup molasses
¼ cup hot cider or water

Stir wheat germ, powdered milk, coconut, and oil together to mix well. Stir in oatmeal. Stir in nuts, sesame and sunflower seeds, and dried fruits. Combine honey, molasses, and cider; pour over fruit mixture, and mix all together well with hands. Spread ½ to 1 inch thick on baking sheets. Bake in a slow oven (325°) for 1 hour or more, until crisp and golden brown, stirring every 5 to 10 minutes and watching carefully to prevent burning. Cool. Package in plastic bags for later use.

Familia   **15 pounds**

You can make this up in smaller quantities; just keep the
same general proportion of ingredients. Four ounces
makes an average serving. For breakfast: Serve with
honey and milk or cream. For trail snacks or lunches:
Add 1 tablespoon powdered milk per 4-ounce serving,
package in plastic bags, and add water at eating time.

2 pounds raisins or currants
2 pounds mixed dried fruits, chopped
1 pound regular rolled oats
2 pounds wheat flakes
2 pounds rye flakes
1 pound wheat germ
1 pound shelled sunflower seeds
1 pound sesame seeds
1 pound soy lecithin
1 pound shredded coconut
1 pound chopped walnuts and almonds (optional)
3 tablespoons ground apple pie spice (or about 6 teaspoons ground cinnamon, 2 teaspoons ground nutmeg,
  and 1 teaspoon ground cloves)
1 tablespoon salt

Mix all ingredients very well. Package in plastic bags for
later use.

Jerky

These recipes tell of two ways to make jerky at home before you go camping. Be sure to use only lean meat. It must be free of fat in order to keep well. Package it tightly in jars or plastic bags for trail or lunch snacks.

In becoming jerky, the meat dries to about one-fourth of its original size and gets crisp and chewy.

I.

5 to 6 pounds lean top or bottom beef round steaks, ½ to ¾ inch thick
Salt
Ground black pepper
Garlic powder

Slice steak into ½-inch-wide strips. Sprinkle with salt, pepper, and garlic powder. Place strips on a rack set over a pan in 200° heat for about 48 hours or until dry; turn once. For heat, use an electric oven, electric roaster, or the pilot of a gas stove. Place a lid or tray over the meat in order to retain the heat of the pilot, yet allow air circulation.

II.

5 to 6 pounds lean beef chuck or round, or lean venison
Soy sauce
Water or dry table wine
Ground black pepper

Slice meat into ½-inch-square strips. Cover with a mixture of equal parts soy and water, and let stand for 1 hour Drain meat well, saving marinade; dry on absorbent paper towels. Sprinkle with black pepper to cover. Place on a rack (set over a pan for catching loose pepper) in a very slow oven (200°) for 24 hours. Baste surfaces with reserved marinade, turn strips, sprinkle again with pepper, and return to oven for 24 hours more or until dry.

Note: Here is a way to try your hand at jerky in camp. Just be sure that someone is in camp at all times while this is going on, or birds and animals will be bound to sample your efforts: Place thin strips of meat or fish on a rack near the campfire — on the smoky side of the fire. Keep it there until meat is nearly dry. Then place in the sunshine away from the fire until thoroughly dry.

Müsli   8 to 10 servings

You eat this as is with milk and honey. Or make it into a hot cereal by adding boiling water in proportions of three parts water to 1 part of cereal mixture.

4 ounces (about 1½ cups) regular rolled oats
4 ounces crushed wheat
4 ounces crushed rye
4 ounces wheat germ
2 ounces raw, shelled sunflower seeds
2 ounces (about ¾ cup) shredded or grated coconut
2 ounces (about ½ cup) chopped nuts
1 teaspoon grated fresh orange or lemon peel

Shortly before trip, mix all ingredients very well. Package in plastic bags.

Lunch Suggestions

In Camp

1. Chili con carne, stew, or soup
2. Omelets with fillings
3. Pancakes with fruit compote
4. Hot cornbread, butter and honey
5. Fresh-caught trout
6. Beef tartare
7. Salad of greens, meat, and cheese
8. Instant potato salad
9. Canned kippers, sardines, or other canned fish
10. Deviled eggs
11. Peanut butter and jelly sandwiches
12. French toast with fruit compote, syrup, or jam
13. Pimento cheese spread sandwiches, toasted or un-toasted
14. Tuna salad or tuna salad sandwiches

On the Trail

1. Salami, beef stick, or jerky (see page 28, or buy "dry" — the nonfat — kind)
2. Small tins of fish or potted meats
3. Slices or chunks of firm cheeses which do not melt easily, such as Cheddar, Gouda, Monterey Jack, Tybo, Norbo, Swiss
4. Deviled eggs
5. Packaged salad mixtures, prepared with only water added, according to package directions
6. Packaged instant applesauce, reconstituted with water
7. Sturdy breads and crackers that travel well, such as

pilot crackers, cocktail thins, rusks, pumpernickel or rye bread, bagels
8. Apples and oranges
9. Freeze-dried and dehydrated fruits of all kinds
10. Freeze-dried cottage cheese (with dried fruits, or alone with salt and pepper)
11. Fruit bars, squares of semi-sweet baking chocolate, or chocolate bars (especially good for winter hiking)
12. Old-fashioned fruitcake (especially good for winter trips)
13. Salted or unsalted nuts
14. Paper-wrapped hard candies, such as lemon drops, coffee chews, peppermints
15. Packaged fruit drink, concentrated and reconstituted, such as lemon, lime, orange, grape
16. Freeze-dried orange juice or grapefruit juice crystals, reconstituted with water
17. Buttermilk (available in dried form)

Soups

Never increase the amount of soup by adding more water. If you must extend a soup, add soup broth — and/or more dried meat, vegetables, herbs, or flavorful fat. Soup should never be thin and watery in flavor; plain hot water is a better beverage.

You should allow at least a 1-cup serving of soup per person. You will need nearly double that amount for night hikers or cold and hungry travelers.

Beyond the basic soup recipes included here, consider the many, many good packaged soups available in markets, mountaineering shops, and gourmet stores. These are tasty, nourishing, and easy to carry for backpacking, river touring, ski touring, or for any other style of camping. You can prepare these packaged soups and improvise upon them in various ways: Expand them with rice, noodles, potatoes, or other starches. Enrich them with any of the freeze-dried or dehydrated vegetables; with barley, peas, beans; with jerky, sausage, ham, fish, fowl, or good red meat. Make them into creamed soups by adding milk. Increase taste intrigue by adding flavoring seeds and herbs (thyme does great things for pea soup, dill adds a spark to potato or tomato soup, cumin makes an exotic out of vegetable-beef soup, a dollop of sherry is good in almost any soup on a cold night). Concoct your own combinations, and do not be afraid to experiment.

Vegetable Soup*

This soup can take on additions such as leftover mashed potatoes (in which case you'll probably want to leave out the barley), other leftover vegetables, or water in which vegetables have been cooked.

About 1 pound beef bones and leftover pieces of meat
4 quarts water
1 teaspoon *each* salt, ground black pepper, and crumbled dried rosemary
1 bay leaf
2 cloves garlic, minced or mashed
1 cup pearl barley
1 large onion, finely chopped
2 or 3 carrots, thinly sliced crosswise
Chopped celery tops from 1 bunch of celery

Put beef bones and meat in a large kettle with water, salt, pepper, rosemary, bay, and garlic. Cover and simmer until meat falls off the bones. Scrape marrow out of bones and return to kettle; discard bones. Add barley, and gently boil for 10 minutes. Add onions, carrots, and celery, and continue cooking until vegetables are tender, about 20 minutes.

*A trail version of Vegetable Soup may be found in *Food for Knapsackers*.

Potato Soup

6 to 8 medium-sized potatoes, peeled and diced
Water
4 tablespoons butter
1 teaspoon salt
½ cup heavy or light cream
1 large onion, minced
1 tablespoon chopped fresh parsley (or about 1 teaspoon
   dried)
1 teaspoon dry mustard
¼ teaspoon cayenne
6 cups milk

In a large kettle, boil potatoes in water to cover until
very tender. Drain. Mash or beat with half of the butter,
the salt, and cream until smooth. In a frying pan, sauté
onion in remaining butter until tender; add to potatoes
along with parsley, mustard, and cayenne. Gradually stir
in milk. Simmer over low heat, stirring, until very hot;
do not allow to boil.

Leek and Potato Soup

6 servings

12 leeks
6 medium-sized potatoes, peeled and diced
6 cups water
4 beef bouillon cubes
1 teaspoon salt
½ teaspoon ground black pepper
1 tablespoon butter

Remove leek roots, outer leaves, and 2 to 3 inches of tops; slice leeks in half lengthwise, and wash very well; thinly slice crosswise. Combine leeks, potatoes, and water in a large kettle. Cover, and gently boil until potatoes are tender. Roughly mash potatoes. Add bouillon cubes, salt, and pepper. Add a little more water if the soup is too thick. Simmer for 5 minutes, then stir in butter.

Minestrone*   **6 servings**

This can be a soup course, or it can be a main dish —
with just a salad and garlic bread to go with it.

1½ pounds ground round or chuck
2 tablespoons olive oil
2 quarts water
1 teaspoon ground black pepper
½ teaspoon salt
⅛ teaspoon crumbled dried rosemary
2 cloves garlic, minced or mashed or 1 tablespoon garlic
   powder
6 ounces (about 1½ cups) macaroni, pasta shells, or
   wagon wheels
1 large onion, finely chopped
1 can (1 pound) stewed tomatoes or tomato wedges
1 small can (8 ounces) kidney beans
1 small can (about 8 ounces) whole-kernel corn
½ to 1 small can (about 8 ounces) green peas
2 teaspoons crumbled dried basil
¼ pound (about 1 cup) grated or shredded Parmesan
   cheese

In a large kettle, brown meat in oil. Add water, pepper,
salt, rosemary, and garlic. Heat to boiling, add macaroni,
cover loosely, and gently boil until macaroni is almost
tender, about 20 minutes. Add onion, tomatoes, beans,
corn, peas, and basil. Simmer until vegetables are well
heated. Pass Parmesan to sprinkle onto soup according
to taste.

*****Food for Knapsackers** contains a trail recipe for Minestrone.*

Meats, Poultry, Fish

Toward increased flavor for freeze-dried meats, poultry, and fish, here are some general suggestions:

Reconstitute freeze-dried item with some seasonings added to the water, rather than with water alone. For example: Reconstitute beef, pork, and lamb in a mixture of half water, half dry red table wine, and some crumbled dried basil, savory, or oregano. Reconstitute chicken, turkey, or fish in a mixture of half water, half dry white table wine, and some crumbled dried tarragon or basil.

Meats and Other Treats for the Skewer and Open Fire

Following are suggestions of meat, fish, vegetable, and fruit combinations to thread on skewers and broil over an open fire. Don't limit the combinations to those listed. The cooking is more fun and more satisfying to each eater if the cook merely provides a selection of ingredients and skewers, and lets each camper choose the ingredients he wishes to thread onto his skewer, cook, and eat.

For each person at this meal, provide at least ½ pound meat and ½ pound *each* of two different fruits or vegetables. Cut meat, vegetables, and fruits into 1½- to 2-inch cubes or slices. Thread on skewers, alternating meat with vegetables or fruits. Baste with olive or other salad oil, or marinate before broiling and baste during broiling with one of the marinades listed on pages 38-40. Cook over coals.

1. Beef, potatoes (parboiled), onions, mushrooms, tomatoes
2. Beef, prawns or lobster tails, mushrooms, onions, tomatoes

3. Beef, oysters wrapped in bacon, celery, onions
4. Lamb, tomatoes, onions, mushrooms
5. Lamb, pork, onions, mushrooms, green-pepper quarters
6. Cooked tongue, ham, chicken or turkey, apple quarters, mushrooms
7. Pork or ham, onions, apple quarters or crab apples
8. Pork or ham, fresh pineapple, mushrooms, bananas
9. Sausages, apples, onions
10. Sausages, bananas wrapped in bacon, apples
11. Hot dogs (canned barbecued), onions, green pepper quarters
12. Salmon, swordfish or other large fish, cucumber, tomatoes
13. Shrimp, scallops or abalone, onions, cucumber, celery
14. Apples, fresh pineapple, bananas, celery
15. Apples, bananas, pitted fresh apricots (a honey marinade is good with these)
16. Eggplant, tomatoes, onions, mushrooms or green-pepper quarters
17. Zucchini, tomatoes, onions, celery
18. Chicken livers basted with oil flavored with garlic and tarragon

Marinades

If foods are to be marinated for only a few hours (as for cooked vegetables, fish, chicken pieces), make the marinade at home and carry it to camp in plastic jars. If foods are to be marinated for 1 or 2 days (as for large roasts, pot roasts, some rabbit), begin marinating at home, and take the meat in marinade to camp in refrigerated boxes or bags. Or securely wrap meat in marinade, freeze it, carry it to camp, and allow it to thaw there.

To use the following marinades: Stir ingredients together. Marinate item in the mixture long enough for flavors to be absorbed, and prepare food item as planned — usually broiled or roasted. Baste with marinade during cooking if you wish.

Marinades suitable for fish, pork, and beef

1. 1 cup soy sauce, 4 tablespoons dry mustard, 4 tablespoons prepared horseradish (optional)
2. 1 cup oil, ½ cup tarragon vinegar, 1 tablespoon mashed capers
3. ½ cup salad oil, ½ cup dry white table wine, 1 tablespoon crumbled dried tarragon
4. ¾ cup dry white table wine, ¼ cup soy sauce, 1 tablespoon grated fresh ginger root (or about 1 teaspoon ground ginger) or 1 tablespoon grated radish

Marinades suitable for beef, lamb, and pork

1. 1 cup salad oil, ½ cup red wine vinegar, 1 tablespoon garlic powder, 1 teaspoon crumbled dried oregano
2. 1 cup white wine vinegar, ½ cup honey, 1 tablespoon sesame seeds
3. ½ cup salad oil, ½ cup red wine vinegar, 1 teaspoon garlic powder, 1 teaspoon crumbled dried basil, 1 teaspoon crumbled dried thyme
4. ½ cup vinegar, ½ cup honey, 1 teaspoon crumbled dried thyme, ½ teaspoon salt, ¼ teaspoon cayenne

Marinade for chicken

3 tablespoons water, 1 tablespoon peanut oil, 1 tablespoon fresh lemon juice, 1 clove garlic, minced or mashed

To use the following marinades: Toss marinade gently with fruits or vegetables which are prepared for eating. That is, vegetables cooked and cut (if necessary), drained canned fruits and vegetables, or raw fruits and vegetables cleaned and sliced.

Marinades suitable for fruits and vegetables

1. ½ cup honey, ¼ cup salad oil, ¼ cup white wine vinegar or lemon juice, about 2 teaspoons mashed capers, and ½ teaspoon crumbled dried tarragon or thyme.
2. ½ cup salad oil, ½ cup white wine vinegar, 1 teaspoon sesame, caraway, or anise seeds
3. For fruit only: ½ cup honey, 1 tablespoon fresh lemon juice, 1 teaspoon wheat germ or grated coconut, 1/8 teaspoon salt

Beef Tartare   1 serving

This is good for lunch with sliced tomatoes sprinkled with oil, vinegar, and capers; and cold beer to drink. Be sure to make and eat Beef Tartare within a few hours of buying the meat.

¼ to ½ pound lean ground round or sirloin
1 egg
¾ cup chopped fresh onion
Dash of Tabasco sauce

On a plate, loosely shape beef into a mound with a depression in center. Break egg into depression. Sprinkle with Tabasco. Arrange onions in a mound beside meat. Eater mixes onions with egg, meat, and more Tabasco according to taste.

Pan Grilled Steak   6 to 8 servings

2-inch thick round beef steak weighing 3 or 4 pounds
Coarse kitchen salt
Black pepper
Butter or blue cheese

Press salt into one side of the steak to coat it thickly.
Place steak, salt side down, in a hot iron frying pan.
Cook over high heat until the salt crusts. Cover the top
side of the steak heavily with salt. Turn steak, and cook
on the second side until salt crusts. With a sharp knife,
make a small cut into steak to check doneness. If you
wish further doneness, turn steak, move frying pan to a
cooler part of the fire, and continue cooking to doneness
you desire. Break off salt crust. Sprinkle meat to season
with salt and pepper. Carve into about 6 to 8 portions.
Top each with a thin slice of butter or blue cheese.

Trail Stew   6 servings

6 ounces freeze-dried potato slices
3 ounces dehydrated onion flakes
1 ounce dehydrated celery flakes
2 quarts water
2 cans (1 pound *each*) beef or 8 ounces freeze-dried
    ground beef or beef chunks
4 tablespoons butter or margarine
1 small dried hot red pepper or ¼ teaspoon crushed
    dried hot peppers
1 tablespoon crumbled dried marjoram
1 teaspoon salt

Put potatoes, onions, celery, and water into a kettle; and
heat to boiling. Add remaining ingredients. Cover, and
simmer for 40 minutes or until potatoes are tender.

Argentine Roast Beef Ribs   5 to 6 servings

A good salad with this: watercress and lettuce with an oil and vinegar dressing.

2 medium-sized onions, finely chopped
2 fresh hot chili peppers, seeds removed, finely chopped
2 tablespoons bacon drippings or cooking oil
1 cup chopped fresh tomatoes or 1 cup drained and
    chopped canned tomatoes
2 cloves garlic, minced or mashed
Beer or dry table wine, if needed
5 to 6 pounds beef short ribs, cut into 2- to 3-inch pieces
Salt and ground black pepper

In a large frying pan or a kettle, sauté onions and peppers in drippings until limp. Add tomatoes and garlic, and simmer, stirring occasionally, until mixture blends to a sauce. If necessary, add a little beer or wine to make sauce of a consistency which will spread easily over meat. Season meat generously with salt and pepper. Place on greased grilling rack over medium coals, turning and basting frequently with sauce, until well browned and tender, at least 30 minutes.

Short Ribs Western   6 servings

3 pounds lean beef short ribs, cut into serving pieces
4 cloves garlic, minced or mashed
1 tablespoon chili powder
1 teaspoon curry powder
About 1 teaspoon salt (to taste)
About 1 cup water
10 ounces dry spaghetti or noodles
6 medium-sized onions, peeled and quartered
1 cup dry red table wine

In a heavy kettle, slowly brown ribs in their own fat.
Add garlic, chili powder, curry powder, salt, and water.
Cover, and simmer until meat is tender, about 2½ hours.
(If necessary to provide enough juices, add more water.)
Add spaghetti and onions. Cover and gently boil until
spaghetti is *al dente* (cooked through, but still slightly
chewy) and onions are slightly cooked yet slightly crisp.
Add wine, and just heat through.

Corned Beef and Cabbage   6 servings

10 ounces dehydrated potato slices
4 ounces dehydrated cabbage flakes
2 ounces dehydrated onion flakes
2 quarts water
4 ounces (½ cup) butter or margarine
1 tablespoon black pepper
1 teaspoon salt
2 cans (1 pound *each*) corned beef

Put potatoes, cabbage, onions, and water into a kettle;
heat to boiling. Add remaining ingredients. Cover, and
simmer until potatoes are tender, about 40 minutes.

43

Flemish Beef Stew

6 servings

Good accompaniments: small boiled potatoes in their jackets, a green salad, cold beer.

2½ pounds lean beef stew meat cut into 1½-inch cubes
Flour
3 tablespoons cooking oil
4 medium-sized onions, thinly sliced
3 tablespoons butter
About 1½ cups beer
1 clove garlic, minced or mashed
1 tablespoon chopped fresh parsley
1 stalk celery, sliced
1 bay leaf
¼ teaspoon crumbled dried thyme
1 tablespoon tarragon-flavored vinegar

Roll meat in flour, and shake off excess. In a heavy kettle, brown meat on all sides in the oil; push to one side of kettle. Add onions, and sauté until limp. In a saucepan, melt butter. Stir in 3 tablespoons flour to make a smooth paste. Gradually add beer, cooking and stirring to make a smooth sauce. Add to kettle along with garlic, parsley, celery, bay leaf, and thyme. Cover and simmer for 2½ hours or until meat is very tender. If necessary to keep sufficient juices during cooking, add a little more beer. Just before serving, add vinegar.

Beef and Oyster Pie   6 servings

If you make this at home, you can cover it with a layer
of pie pastry or a very thin layer of rolled-out biscuit
dough, and bake it. Use a hot oven (425°) for about 10
minutes, then reduce oven heat to moderate (350°) and
bake for about 30 minutes more or until crust is brown.

¼ pound fresh mushrooms, sliced
About 2 tablespoons olive oil
2 tablespoons flour
1 teaspoon salt
½ teaspoon ground black pepper
½ cup milk
1 tablespoon crumbled dried summer savory
2 pounds lean beef stew meat, cut into ¾-inch cubes
2 pints fresh or canned oysters, drained
2 medium-sized potatoes, peeled and coarsely grated
1 medium-sized onion, finely chopped
2 tablespoons chopped fresh parsley

In a frying pan, sauté mushrooms in about 1 tablespoon
of the oil until tender; remove from pan. Add enough
more oil to pan to make 2 tablespoons liquid; stir in
flour, salt and pepper to make a smooth paste. Gradually
add milk, cooking and stirring until sauce is smooth and
thickened; stir in summer savory and mushrooms. Arrange half of the beef over bottom of a heavy kettle, top
with half of the oysters, half of the potatoes, half of the
onion, and half of the mushroom sauce. Repeat layering
to use remaining half of ingredients. Sprinkle with parsley. Cover and simmer for 30 to 45 minutes or until
meat and potatoes are tender.

Sonofabitch Stew

This is an old-time cow-camp stew. Nowadays, sour cream serves in place of the former marrow gut ingredient (the stomach of a nursing calf). Good accompaniments: green salad, hot garlic bread, red wine.

¾ pound fresh beef tongue or lamb tongue, simmered in water to cover until tender
¾ pound beef heart or lamb heart, simmered in water to cover until tender
1½ pounds lean boneless beef stew meat, cut into 1-inch cubes
½ pound oxtails
4 tablespoons beef suet, chopped
6 cloves garlic, minced or mashed
6 dried chili *tepines* or about 1½ teaspoons crushed dried hot red peppers
About 1 tablespoon ground black pepper
About 1 teaspoon salt (to taste)
1 teaspoon crumbled dried marjoram
1 teaspoon crumbled dried thyme
Water
1 beef brain (2 sections), washed and membrane removed
1 cup commercial sour cream, or sour cream reconstituted from powder, or imitation sour cream
6 tablespoons chopped fresh parsley

Remove skin from tongue; cut tongue into 1-inch cubes. Remove any fat or arteries from heart; cut heart into 1-inch cubes. In a heavy kettle, brown tongue, heart, stew meat, and oxtails in suet. Add garlic, chili *tepines*, pepper, salt, marjoram, thyme, and enough water to cover bottom of kettle by about ½ inch. Cover, and simmer for 1 hour or until meat is tender. (If necessary, add a little more water during cooking.) Remove oxtail bones and discard. Cut brains into 1-inch pieces, add to kettle, cover, and simmer for about 15 minutes more. Just before serving, stir in sour cream and parsley.

Beef with Mushrooms 6 servings

Good accompaniments: sliced tomatoes and Golden Rice (page 112).

2 pounds beef round steak, cut into very thin strips
½ cup soy sauce
About 4 tablespoons butter
1 large onion, finely chopped
¾ pound fresh mushrooms, thinly sliced
½ cup commercial sour cream

Turn meat in soy, and let stand, chilled, for 1 hour. In a large, heavy frying pan, melt butter over medium-high heat. Lift meat from soy, add to pan, and brown quickly; push to one side of pan, add onion and mushrooms, and sauté until limp. Return drained soy to pan. Cover, and simmer until meat is tender. Just before serving, stir in sour cream.

Variation: Freeze-dried version: substitute 6 ounces freeze-dried ground beef for round steak. Substitute 1½ ounces freeze-dried or dehydrated onion flakes for fresh onion. Substitute 3 ounces freeze-dried mushrooms for fresh. Soak beef, onions, and mushrooms until soft in enough water just to cover and enough soy to season. Drain. Prepare as above, *except* finish with 3 ounces packaged powdered sour cream sauce, reconstituted.

Mincemeat

You do not make this in camp; you make it weeks before at home. This recipe makes a large batch, so you will probably want to take only about half of it on your camping trip. Use the rest for pies at home.

3-pound beef tongue, boiled until tender, peeled and
    trimmed and finely chopped
1½ pounds beef suet, finely chopped
2 pounds (4½ cups) sugar
1 pound seedless raisins
1 pound dried currants
3 pounds apples, peeled cored and finely chopped
4 ounces citron, finely chopped
4 ounces candied orange peel, finely chopped
4 ounces (about 1 cup) finely chopped almonds
2 teaspoons salt
1½ teaspoons *each* ground cinnamon, cloves, allspice and
    nutmeg
Grated peel and juice of 2 oranges
Grated peel and juice of 2 lemons
4 cups brandy
2 cups bourbon

Combine all ingredients except oranges, lemons, brandy and bourbon in a large crock or crockery jar with a cover. Mix thoroughly. Combine orange and lemon peels and juice, brandy, bourbon and pour over fruit mixture. Cover with a clean cloth, then with the lid of the crock. Keep in a cool place for about 3 weeks. Stir well.

To prepare mincemeat for camp lunches: Heat to boiling, then simmer uncovered until liquid has evaporated and the mixture is thick. Stir occasionally. Cool. Put into 6- or 8-ounce plastic bags or cartons. Refrigerate or chill until used.

For mince pies: Refrigerate until ready to use. Mince-meat will keep indefinitely in the refrigerator.

Hash   6 to 8 servings

For breakfast, serve with a poached egg on top of each serving. For dinner, serve with a green salad or hot green vegetable accompanying it.

3 pounds canned and coarsely chopped roast beef or
    leftover roast beef, roast pork, cooked heart, boiled
    tongue, or canned roast beef
3 onions, chopped
2 raw potatoes, peeled and chopped
2 cloves garlic, minced or mashed
4 small dried hot red peppers, crushed, or about ½ tea-
    spoon crushed hot dried red peppers
About 1 tablespoon ground black pepper
About 1 teaspoon salt (to taste)
1 teaspoon crumbled dried oregano or marjoram
1 teaspoon ground cumin *(comino)*
Water

Combine all ingredients except water in a large frying pan. Add enough water to almost cover all ingredients, and cook over low heat until potatoes and onions are tender, about 30 minutes. Stir occasionally; add a little more water if necessary to prevent drying out or burning. When finished, hash should be moist but with all excess liquid cooked away.

Hekka

Serve this over hot rice. Good accompaniments: Chinese
Cabbage (or other cabbage) Salad (page 129), pineapple
spears, and cookies.

2 pounds beef sirloin tip, very thinly sliced
About 4 tablespoons peanut oil
1¼ cups soy sauce
¼ cup brown sugar, firmly packed
½ pound fresh mushrooms (or use 1 cup drained canned
    mushrooms or 4 ounces dried mushrooms which have
    been soaked until tender, and sliced)
1 can (8 ounces) bamboo shoots, drained
About 15 green onions with tops, cut into 1-inch lengths
2 stalks celery, sliced diagonally into 1-inch lengths
2- by 2- by 1-inch block of bean curd (Tofu)

In a large frying pan, brown meat quickly over high heat
in peanut oil. Add soy and sugar, and cook and stir for
about 3 minutes, until reduced slightly. Add mushrooms, bamboo shoots, onions, and celery. Cook, lightly
stirring, just until tender-crisp. Add bean curd, stir well
to break up and mix, and serve immediately.

Korean Beef and Mushrooms   6 servings

Good accompaniments: buttered noodles and Chinese Cabbage Salad (page 129).

2 pounds ground beef round
Cooking oil
½ pound fresh mushrooms, thinly sliced (or 4 ounces dried mushrooms which have been soaked until tender, drained, and sliced)
4 green onions with part of green tops, thinly sliced
2 cloves garlic, minced or mashed
2 tablespoons sesame seeds
1 teaspoon grated fresh ginger root or 1 teaspoon minced candied ginger or about ¼ teaspoon ground dried ginger
1 teaspoon salt
About ¼ teaspoon ground black pepper
1 cup water
6 tablespoons soy sauce
3 eggs, slightly beaten

In a large, heavy frying pan, brown meat over medium-high heat in a small amount of oil. Add remaining ingredients except eggs, and cook and stir until just tender. Just before serving, add eggs, and stir just until mixed and barely cooked.

Beef or Lamb Curry (Cream Style) 6 servings

Serve over Golden Rice (page 112). Offer these condiments, each in a small bowl, surrounding a larger bowl of Camper's Chutney (page 154, or use commercial mango chutney): 2/3 cup raisins, 2/3 cup chopped walnuts or other nuts, 2/3 cup dehydrated banana flakes, ½ cup shredded or flaked coconut, ½ cup plain yogurt, and 3 or 4 slices bacon which have been crisply cooked and crumbled. Eaters add condiments to curry according to taste.

¼ cup butter or margarine
4 tablespoons flour
2 tablespoons curry powder
2 teaspoons ground coriander
1 teaspoon salt
1 teaspoon turmeric
3 cups milk
1½ pounds cooked beef or lamb, diced (or 6 ounces
    freeze-dried turkey or chicken which has been soaked
    in water to cover for 15 minutes)

In a large saucepan or frying pan, melt butter. Stir in flour, curry powder, coriander, salt, and turmeric to make a smooth paste. Gradually add milk, and cook and stir over low heat to make a smooth and thickened sauce. Add beef or lamb (or reconstituted freeze-dried chicken or turkey with its water). Simmer for several minutes to heat through and blend seasonings.

Hamburger and Potato Cakes   6 servings

For breakfast or dinner.

6 ounces freeze-dried ground beef
3 ounces freeze-dried onion flakes
Water
1 tablespoon dehydrated parsley flakes
1 teaspoon salt
1 teaspoon ground black or red pepper
10 ounces instant mashed potato flour or flakes
Boiling water
Butter or margarine

Barely cover beef and onions with water, and let soak until soft. Add parsley, salt, and pepper. Mix potatoes and boiling water according to package directions for mashed potatoes. Stir in 3 tablespoons of the butter and beef and onions with soaking juices. (Mixture should be stiff.) Shape mixture into round or rectangular patties about ½ to ¾ inch thick (use about ½ cup of the mixture for each patty.) Brown patties on both sides in butter on medium-hot griddle or in a skillet.

Meat Ball Pancakes

6 servings

You should serve these just as soon as they are baked —
as they are for breakfast, or topped with Mushroom
Sauce (page 153) or other creamed vegetables for dinner.

3 eggs, separated
½ pound ground beef
1 tablespoon grated fresh onion
1 tablespoon chopped fresh parsley
½ teaspoon salt
¼ teaspoon baking powder
¼ teaspoon ground black pepper
1 teaspoon fresh lemon juice

Beat egg yolks slightly, and stir in meat and all remaining
ingredients except egg whites. Beat egg whites until stiff
but not dry, and fold into mixture. Drop by tablespoonfuls onto a greased hot griddle. When cakes are puffed
and browned on one side, turn and brown on second
side.

Texas Chili con Carne

For lunch: Serve the chili without beans, and with saltines and cold beer. For dinner: Add the beans, and serve chili with a green salad and beer or wine. Chili is better if you make it one day, chill, and reheat for serving the second day.

3 pounds beef, chopped or coarsely ground
2 ounces beef suet, finely chopped
About 4 tablespoons chili powder
2 teaspoons salt
4 cloves garlic, minced or mashed
3 tablespoons crumbled dried oregano
1 tablespoon ground cumin *(comino)*
2 tablespoons corn meal or *masa harina**
2 to 4 cups chili beans (or use 1 or 2 1-pound cans of
    pinto beans) (optional)

In a large, heavy frying pan or kettle, brown the beef and suet. Add chili powder, salt, and garlic. Heat to boiling, then simmer, covered, for 30 minutes. Add oregano, cumin, and corn meal; and simmer for 1 hour more. Allow chili to cool, and remove excess grease if you wish. (If you wish, add chili beans.) Reheat before serving.

If you like a hotter, spicier chili, add these along with the cumin and oregano: 3 additional tablespoons chili powder, 1 tablespoon cayenne, and more garlic cloves.

*Finely ground Mexican corn meal used especially for making tortillas and tamales.

Tamale Pie*

6 to 8 servings

2 pounds ground lean beef
Bacon drippings
2 onions, chopped
1 green bell pepper, chopped
1 can (8 ounces) tomato sauce
1 can (8 ounces) whole-kernel corn, drained
4 tablespoons chili powder
1½ teaspoons salt
1 teaspoon ground cumin *(comino)*
1 teaspoon crumbled dried oregano
2 cups yellow corn meal
1 cup dry powdered milk
2 teaspoons salt
2 cups water
About 15 pitted ripe olives
½ teaspoon cayenne

In a heavy frying pan or kettle, lightly brown meat in a small amount of bacon drippings. Stir in onions and pepper, and cook until limp. Add tomato sauce, corn, chili powder, the 1½ teaspoons salt, cumin, and oregano. Simmer for about 10 minutes, stirring occasionally. Meantime, prepare corn meal mixture: In a saucepan, mix corn meal, dry milk, and the 2 teaspoons salt; gradually stir in water. Cook and stir over low heat until mixture thickens and bubbles, about 10 to 15 minutes. Spread half of the corn meal mixture over bottom of a greased Dutch oven (in camp) or baking pan (at home). Spoon meat mixture evenly over top. Sprinkle with olives. Spoon remaining corn meal mixture over top. Sprinkle with cayenne. In camp: Cover Dutch oven,

*A trail version of this dish may be found in *Food for Knapsackers.*

56

bury in coals, and bake for about 20 minutes. At home: Bake, uncovered, in a moderate oven (350°) for about 30 minutes.

Enchiladas   6 servings

If you want plump enchiladas (and 1 per person), use 6 tortillas. If you want skinnier enchiladas (and 2 per person), use 12 tortillas. If you have some Chili con Carne made up and available (recipe page 55, or other chili con carne), you can use that as the filling for these enchiladas instead of the following ground beef mixture. Good enchilada accompaniments: Beans with Cheese (page 115), Salsa Caliente (page 153), and cold beer or wine.

2 pounds ground beef
3 large onions, chopped
2 tablespoons finely chopped green bell peppers
1 large clove garlic, minced or mashed
1 tablespoon cayenne
1 tablespoon bacon drippings
6 or 12 tortillas
1 pound Monterey Jack or sharp Cheddar cheese, shred-
    ded or thinly sliced

In a large frying pan, lightly cook together beef, onions, pepper, garlic, and cayenne in bacon drippings until meat is crumbly and onions are limp. For each enchila-da: Spoon 1/6 (or 1/12) of the meat mixture down center of tortilla, roll up and place in a greased shallow pan, seam side down. Repeat, using all tortillas and meat mixture. Top with cheese. Cover pan and place on or near campfire until enchiladas heat through and cheese melts (or slip under oven broiler until cheese melts and browns).

Letters from Home   **2 servings**

You make these at home and take them to camp.

1 cup flour
½ teaspoon salt
1/3 cup lard, vegetable shortening, or margarine
1 to 2 tablespoons cold water
½ pound ground beef round
1 medium-sized potato, cut into ¼-inch dices
1 medium-sized onion, chopped
Tabasco sauce
Salt and ground black pepper
2 tablespoons butter

Sift or stir together flour and salt in a mixing bowl. Cut
in shortening until particles are about the size of small
peas. Add just enough water to moisten, toss with a fork
to mix, and gather into a ball. On a lightly floured
board, roll out to a 10- by 9-inch rectangle. Cut in half
to make two 9- by 5-inch rectangles. Layer in the center
of the upper half of each rectangle one-fourth of the
meat, half of the potato, half of the onion, one-fourth of
the meat, a dash of Tabasco, salt and pepper to taste,
and dots of half of the butter. Fold up bottom half of
pastry to cover meat mixture. Pinch edges together to
seal well. Prick top with a fork. Place on ungreased
baking sheet. Bake in a moderate oven (350°) for 1 hour
or until golden brown.

Variation: Use packaged pie pastry mix for a 1-crust pie
instead of pastry above.

Cornish Pasties

You make these at home, and take them to camp. But they must be eaten while hot — by hand. To reheat at camp: Place in oiled Dutch oven, cover, and set into low coals. The suet is the major part of the pastry shortening because it gives a particularly flaky texture. The pastry will be slightly more moist than usual pie pastry.

3 cups flour
1 teaspoon salt
¼ cup lard or margarine
1 cup finely chopped beef suet
6 to 7 tablespoons cold water
1 pound lean beef, finely diced
½ pound lean pork, finely diced
Salt and ground black pepper
2 small uncooked potatoes, peeled and thinly sliced
2 small uncooked turnips, thinly sliced
1 medium-sized onion, chopped
About 4 teaspoons butter

Sift or stir together flour and salt in a mixing bowl. Cut in shortening until particles are fine. Stir in suet. Add water to moisten, toss with a fork to mix, and gather into a ball. Divide into 4 parts. Mix beef and pork with salt and pepper to season. For each pasty: On a lightly floured board, roll a portion of the dough into an 8- or 9-inch circle. Layer over upper half of circle ¼ of the potatoes, salt and pepper to season, ¼ of the turnips, ¼ of the onion, and ¼ of the meat mixture. Dot with ¼ of the butter. Fold lower half of pastry up to cover filling. Pinch edges together to seal well. Prick surfaces with a fork or cut several small slashes. Place on a baking sheet. Bake in a moderate oven (375°) for 1 hour or more, until well browned.

Cousin Jack Pasty

4 servings

Bake at home; take to camp. Serve hot. Eat by hand.

3 cups flour
1 teaspoon salt
¼ cup lard or margarine
1 cup finely chopped beef suet
6 to 7 tablespoons cold water
1½ cups finely diced uncooked potatoes
1½ pounds beef round steak, cut into ¼-inch cubes
2 large onions, thinly sliced
½ teaspoon crumbled dried oregano
½ teaspoon crumbled dried basil
Salt and ground black pepper
3 tablespoons butter

Sift or stir together flour and salt in a mixing bowl. Cut in shortening until particles are fine. Stir in suet. Add water to moisten, toss with a fork to mix, and gather into a ball. Divide into 4 parts. For each pasty: On a lightly floured board, roll a portion of the dough into an 8- or 9-inch circle. Layer over upper half of circle ¼ of the potatoes, ¼ of the meat, ¼ of the onions, ¼ of the oregano and basil, and salt and pepper to season. Dot with ¼ of the butter. Fold lower half of pastry up to cover filling. Pinch edges together to seal well. Prick surface with a fork or cut several small slashes. Place on a baking sheet. Bake in a moderate oven (375°) for 1 hour or more, until well browned.

Variation: Substitute packaged pie pastry mix for 3 1-crust pies for pastry above.

Spaghetti and Beef Sauce*

6 to 7 servings

Good accompaniments: green salad with anchovies and oil and vinegar dressing, celery sticks, garlic bread, and red wine.

2 pounds ground beef
1 tablespoon olive oil
1 medium-sized onion, chopped
1 can (6 ounces) tomato paste
1 clove garlic, minced or mashed
1 tablespoon crumbled dried oregano
Salt
¼ teaspoon crumbled dried rosemary
2 tablespoons finely chopped green bell pepper
2 tablespoons chopped celery tops
¼ pound sliced mushrooms (fresh or canned)
Water
12 ounces dry spaghetti
¼ pound shredded or grated Parmesan or Romano
    cheese

In a large kettle or frying pan, cook meat in olive oil until brown and crumbly. Add onion, sauté until limp. Stir in tomato paste, garlic, oregano, about 1½ teaspoons salt, rosemary, green pepper, celery tops, mushrooms, and 1 cup water. Cover and simmer, stirring occasionally, until blended to a sauce, about 30 minutes. (Add a little water as necessary to make a good thick-sauce consistency.) Correct seasoning. Drop spaghetti into a kettle generously filled with boiling salted water. Boil *al dente* (until cooked through, but still slightly chewy). Drain well. Top with the sauce, sprinkle with cheese, and serve immediately.

*For trail version, see Italian Spaghetti in *Food for Knapsackers*.

Tripe and Dumplings

6 servings

If you prefer to make dumplings yourself rather than using this canned-biscuit version, see recipe on page 148.

1 honeycomb tripe (1½ to 2 pounds)
1 cup finely chopped smoked ham
2 cups dry white table wine
½ cup water
2 onions, chopped
4 to 5 stalks celery, chopped
1 cup chopped fresh parsley
1 tablespoon crumbled dried chervil (an herb)
1 teaspoon crumbled dried thyme
1 bay leaf
1 package (10) refrigerator biscuits
About 1 tablespoon butter
Paprika

Wash tripe well in several changes of cold water. Cut into 1- by ½-inch strips. Put into a heavy kettle with wine and water. Cover, and simmer for 2 hours. Add onions, celery, parsley, chervil, thyme and bay. Cover, and simmer until tripe is tender, about 30 minutes more. Cut each biscuit in half, and arrange on top of bubbling stew. Dot each with butter and sprinkle generously with paprika. Cover kettle tightly, and simmer for 20 minutes or until dumplings are done. (To test, break open one dumpling to see if it is cooked through.)

Tripe and Onion Stew   6 servings

3 pounds honeycomb tripe
2 whole carrots, peeled
3 celery leaves
3 sprigs parsley
2 whole cloves
6 whole peppercorns
1 bay leaf
About 1 teaspoon salt
Water
20 small boiling onions
Boiling salted water
3 tablespoons butter
3 tablespoons flour
1½ cups milk
2 tablespoons fresh lemon juice

Wash tripe well in several changes of cold water. Cut into 1- by 1½-inch pieces. Place in a heavy kettle or Dutch oven with carrots, celery leaves, parsley, cloves, peppercorns, bay, and salt. Add cold water to cover. Cover, and simmer for 2 hours. Drain off liquid; strain and save 1½ cups. Meantime, cook onions, uncovered, in boiling salted water until tender, about 20 minutes; drain. In a saucepan, melt butter. Stir in flour to make a smooth paste. Gradually add milk and reserve tripe liquid, cooking and stirring until sauce is smooth and thickened. Add tripe and onions, mix well, and simmer for a few minutes more. Stir in lemon juice.

Venison Steaks

6 servings

6 venison steaks, each 2 inches thick
2 tablespoons cooking oil
4 tablespoons butter
1 teaspoon salt
1 teaspoon Worcestershire sauce
1 tablespoon fresh lemon juice
2 tablespoons chopped fresh parsley

Rub steak surfaces with cooking oil. Place on greased grill over medium-hot coals. Broil, turning several times, until done, about 10 minutes total for rare. In a small pan, melt butter, stir in remaining ingredients, heat through, pour over broiled steaks.

Venison Hawaiian

6 servings

12 ½-inch-thick venison steaks
2 cups soy sauce
6 cloves garlic, minced or mashed
2 tablespoons sugar or honey
1 teaspoon cayenne

Put steaks into a large bowl. Stir together soy, garlic, sugar, and cayenne, and pour over steaks. Cover, chill, and let marinate for 24 hours; turn occasionally. Barbecue steaks over medium-low charcoal, turning once, and brushing with marinade. Or grill in a very small amount of shortening over medium-low heat on a griddle or in a heavy frying pan.

Variation: Do not marinate steaks. Just broil or grill, season with salt and pepper, and serve with the following sauce ladled over: Stir together in a saucepan 2 tablespoons butter, 2 tablespoons guava or apple jelly, 2 tablespoons dry red table wine, and 1 tablespoon dry mustard. Cook and stir over low heat until blended.

Venison Stew

3 pounds boneless venison meat, cut into about 1-inch
   cubes
3 cups wine vinegar
3 tablespoons whole mixed pickling spices
1 tablespoon salt
1 bay leaf
1 onion, chopped
1 tablespoon flour
1 tablespoon garlic powder (or to taste)
¼ cup dry red table wine or water
1 tablespoon melted butter

Put meat into a large bowl. Stir together vinegar, pickling spices, salt, bay leaf, and onion; and pour over meat.
Cover, chill, and let marinate for 24 hours; turn occasionally. Put meat with marinade into a heavy kettle,
cover, and simmer for 3 hours or until meat is tender.
Stir together flour, garlic powder, wine, and butter to
make a paste. Stir into bubbling stew juices. Simmer for
5 to 10 minutes more, stirring occasionally, until juices
are slightly thickened.

Hunter's Stew I

3 pounds lean beef stew meat or venison steaks, cut into
   ¾-inch cubes
1 tablespoon flour
1 teaspoon salt
4 tablespoons bacon drippings
1 bunch green onions, cut into 2-inch lengths
3 stalks celery, cut diagonally into 2-inch lengths
1 pound fresh mushrooms (or use about 2 cups drained
   canned mushrooms, or 4 ounces dried mushrooms
   which have been soaked until tender and chopped)
½ cup dry red table wine
6 tablespoons soy sauce
1 tablespoon grated fresh ginger root (or use about 1
   teaspoon ground ginger)
1 teaspoon cayenne

Mix flour and salt; add meat, and turn to coat with
seasoned flour. In a heavy kettle, brown meat in bacon
drippings. Arrange onions, celery, and mushrooms on
top of meat. Stir together wine, soy, ginger, and cayenne, and pour over meat. Cover, and simmer for 1 hour
or until meat is tender.

Hunter's Stew II

8 servings

Good accompaniments: hot corn bread and butter and baked apples with whipped cream.

1½ to 2 pounds lean venison, lamb or beef stew meat, cut into 1-inch cubes
Oil
1 large can (15 ounces) tomato sauce
2 onions, chopped
3 stalks celery, chopped
1 green bell pepper, chopped
1 clove garlic, minced or mashed
1 tablespoon salt
1 tablespoon crumbled dried oregano
1 teaspoon ground black pepper
Pinch of crumbled dried rosemary
1 pound yellow squash, cut into ¾-inch cubes
1 package (10 ounces) frozen lima beans

In a heavy kettle or Dutch oven, brown meat in a small amount of oil. Add tomato sauce, onions, celery, green pepper, garlic, salt, oregano, pepper, and rosemary. Cover and simmer for 1½ hours. Add squash and beans; cover and simmer for 30 minutes more or until tender.

Spicy Lamb Stew   6 to 8 servings

3 pounds boneless lean lamb, cut into 1½-inch chunks
3 tablespoons butter
2 onions, thinly sliced
1 teaspoon *each* salt, black pepper, celery salt, and
   ground cinnamon
½ teaspoon crumbled dried thyme
1 can (1 pound) tomatoes (stewed, peeled whole, or
   wedges)
1 cup dry white table wine
2 tablespoons flour
4 small unpeeled apples, cut in eighths and cores removed
1 cup green peas (fresh or frozen)
1 cup peeled and sliced carrots

In a heavy kettle, brown lamb in butter. Add onions,
and sauté until limp. Add salt, pepper, celery salt, cinnamon, thyme, tomatoes, and wine. Cover and simmer 1
hour or until meat is tender. Drain liquid off meat into a
saucepan. Stir together about 4 tablespoons of the liquid
and the flour until smooth. Heat liquid to bubbling.
Gradually add flour mixture, stirring. Continue cooking,
stirring, until liquid is smooth and slightly thickened to a
sauce. Arrange apples, peas, and carrots over meat; pour
sauce over. Cover and simmer until vegetables are tender,
about 10 minutes.

Irish Stew

Serve this with buttered noodles, mashed potatoes, or Dumplings (page 148).

¼ cup flour
2 teaspoons salt
½ teaspoon black pepper
3 pounds boneless lamb shoulder, cut into 1½-inch cubes
3 tablespoons shortening
½ cup finely chopped onions
3 cloves of garlic, minced or mashed
2 teaspoons celery seed
3 cups water
6 to 8 whole carrots, peeled and halved, crosswise
12 small boiling onions, peeled
2 tablespoons chopped fresh parsley (or dried parsley)
2 tablespoons Worcestershire sauce

Mix flour, salt, and pepper; add meat and turn to coat with seasoned flour, and shake off excess. In a heavy kettle, brown meat in shortening. Stir in chopped onions and garlic. Add any remaining seasoned flour, the celery seed, and water. Cover and simmer for 1 hour or until meat is tender. Add carrots and boiling onions; cover and simmer until tender, about 20 minutes. Stir in Worcestershire and parsley.

Variation: Add 2 or 3 peeled and quartered potatoes or 6 small unpeeled new potatoes along with carrots.

Soesatie ("Su-<u>sa</u>-tee") 6 to 7 servings

Good dinner accompaniments: sweet potatoes, a green salad, chilled dry rosé or white wine, and fruit and cheese.

2 pounds lean lamb, cut into 1½- to 2-inch cubes
2 pounds lean pork, cut into 1½- to 2-inch cubes
1 large onion, chopped
1 tablespoon shortening
1 large clove garlic, minced or mashed
1 tablespoon salt
About 2 teaspoons curry powder
½ teaspoon cayenne
1 can (1 pound) apricots, drained and finely chopped (or
    use 1½ cups cooked dried apricots sweetened with 1
    tablespoon honey, finely chopped)
1 cup wine or cider vinegar

In frying pan, sauté onion in shortening until tender. Stir in garlic, salt, curry powder, cayenne, and apricots. Remove from heat, add lamb and pork, gently turn to coat meat well with onion mixture. Turn into a crock or ceramic bean pot with lid. Gently pour vinegar over top to form a sealing film. Cover loosely and refrigerate or keep in a very cool place for 2 days. Stir to mix. To cook: Thread meat cubes on skewers, alternating lamb and pork. Broil over medium heat of an open fire or charcoal until well done. Turn frequently; be careful not to burn the sauce by overcooking or cooking over too high a heat.

Wine-Marinated Steak or Shish Kebabs   6 servings

You can also use this mixture of wine and seasoning to make marinated mushrooms for hors d'oeuvre: Simply marinate mushroom caps in the mixture for 8 hours or overnight.

½ cup dry red table wine
½ cup salad oil
2 tablespoons catsup
1 tablespoon vinegar
1 clove garlic, minced or mashed
1 teaspoon Worcestershire sauce
1 teaspoon sugar
½ teaspoon *each* salt and crumbled dried rosemary and
    marjoram
About 2 pounds steak for broiling (or boneless lean lamb
    cut into cubes for shish kebabs)

Mix together well all ingredients except beef or lamb. Pour mixture over steak or lamb, and allow to stand for 2 hours. Broil steaks over fire; or thread lamb onto skewers, and broil over fire.

Beans and Ham   6 servings

1 pound (2 cups) dry pinto or red beans
½ pound smoked ham or cured pork shoulder, diced
2 tablespoons brown sugar
2 tablespoons dry mustard
1 teaspoon salt
Water

Place beans, ham, sugar, mustard, and salt in a large kettle. Add enough water to cover well. Cover and simmer until beans are tender, about 3 hours. If necessary, add more water during cooking.

Sweet-and-Sour Pork Steaks 6 servings

Be sure to simmer over *low* heat; and watch carefully to prevent burning, adding a little more water as needed. Good accompaniments: sweet potatoes, buttered green peas, Fruit Salad (see page 136), and pound cake.

6 tablespoons cornstarch
2 teaspoons salt
6 tablespoons soy sauce
6 1-inch-thick boneless pork steaks, 8 ounces *each*
Shortening
2 cups cider or wine vinegar
1 cup honey
2 tablespoons minced or grated fresh ginger root (or use about 1½ teaspoons ground ginger)
2 cups canned unsweetened pineapple juice
2 cups water
1 can (1 pound 4 ounces) crushed pineapple, slightly drained, or 2 cups finely chopped fresh pineapple

Stir together cornstarch, salt, and soy; spread over both sides of steaks. In a large, heavy, frying pan or kettle, brown steaks on both sides in a small amount of shortening. Add remaining ingredients except pineapple. Cover, and simmer for about 20 minutes. Turn steaks, and add a little water if liquid has evaporated. Cover and cook for about 30 minutes more or until steaks are tender. Add pineapple, and heat just through.

Variation: Prepare 8 pounds pork spareribs, cracked and cut into serving-size pieces, in the same way. Makes 4 to 5 servings.

Ham Slices   6 servings

1½ pounds lean boneless ham slices, cut ½-inch thick
1 cup milk
1 tablespoon dry mustard

Trim any fat off ham, and use it as shortening to quickly
and lightly brown ham in a heavy frying pan. Stir milk
and mustard together, and pour over ham. Cover, and
simmer for a few minutes, until ham is tender; turn
once.

Baked Ham with Guava and Sherry   6 servings

Good accompaniments: sweet potatoes, Chinese Cabbage Salad (see page 129), and Fruit Salad (page 136) or
pineapple spears.

3-pound canned ham
1 cup dry or medium-dry sherry
½ cup guava jelly
1 teaspoon grated fresh ginger root or about ¼ teaspoon
    ground ginger
4 thin lemon slices
2 tablespoons cornstarch
2 tablespoons water

Drain juices from canned ham, and mix with the sherry,
jelly, and ginger. Place ham in heavy kettle or Dutch
oven. Pour sherry mixture over, and arrange lemon slices
over ham. Place over low heat, cover, and heat thoroughly, about 30 minutes. Baste occasionally with sherry
juices. Remove ham from pan, and carve. Stir together
cornstarch and water to make a smooth paste, add to
pan juices, and cook and stir until thickened slightly and
clear; serve as a sauce over ham slices.

Ham and Oyster Pie   6 to 7 servings

1½ pounds cooked ham, cut into 2-inch cubes.
2 tablespoons butter
2 tablespoons flour
1½ cups milk
About 1 teaspoon salt
1 teaspoon crumbled dried marjoram
½ teaspoon ground black pepper
2 pints fresh or canned oysters
1 package (10 ounces) frozen peas
2 cups packaged biscuit mix

Place ham in Dutch oven; place over low heat to heat through. In a saucepan, melt butter. Stir in flour to make a smooth paste. Gradually add ½ cup milk, cooking and stirring over low heat to make a smooth, thick sauce. Stir in salt, marjoram, and pepper. Drain off any juices which have accumulated with ham. Add oysters, peas, and sauce to ham; turn gently to mix. Stir together biscuit mix and 1 cup milk; spoon evenly over ham mixture. Cover Dutch oven, bury in coals, and bake for about 40 minutes.

Black-Eyed Peas

This recipe is for black-eyed peas as a main dish with just salad and dessert accompanying. You can also cook the recipe the same way, minus the meat, and serve it as an accompaniment to meat or as a protein main dish for vegetarians. Either way, the dish is soupy — about two cups of liquid will remain unabsorbed at end of cooking.

½ to ¾ pound meaty smoked ham hock or ¼ pound salt pork
1 pound (about 2¼ cups) dried black-eyed peas
8 to 9 cups water
About 1 tablespoon salt
1 teaspoon ground black pepper
2 tablespoons crumbled dried oregano or about 1 teaspoon snipped fresh oregano leaves

Score ham hock to cut skin and meat to the bone; score salt pork to the skin. Rinse peas. Combine meat, peas, and water in a kettle. Heat to boiling, then cover and simmer for 30 minutes. Add remaining ingredients, cover, and continue to simmer until beans are tender and beginning to break apart, about 15 minutes more.

Here is another simple way of preparing black-eyed peas: Cook packaged frozen peas according to package directions *except* add to the cooking water salt, pepper, and oregano to season. Season cooked peas with butter. Serve as a vegetable alongside meat.

Golden Risotto   6 servings

½ pound cured pork shoulder or boiled ham, chopped
¼ pound dried shrimp
½ ounce dehydrated onion flakes or 1 medium-sized
    onion, chopped
½ ounce dried mushrooms, broken into bits or 3 ounces
    fresh or canned mushrooms
About 2 teaspoons concentrated seasoned chicken stock
    base
½ teaspoon soy sauce
1/8 teaspoon ground saffron or turmeric
Water
½ pound (about 2½ cups) packaged precooked (instant)
    rice
Shredded or grated Parmesan cheese

In a large kettle or Dutch oven, combine ham, shrimp,
onions, mushrooms, chicken stock base, soy, saffron,
and enough water to cover. Boil for 1 or 2 minutes, until
dried ingredients are reconstituted. Add enough water to
make 2½ cups liquid in kettle. Sprinkle in rice, and
return to boiling. Cover, remove from heat, and let stand
for 10 minutes or until rice is tender. Serve sprinkled
with Parmesan.

Garlic Sausage and Sauerkraut   6 servings

6 or more garlic sausages
6 small unpeeled boiling potatoes
1 tablespoon dill seed
1 teaspoon salt
Water
1 large can (1 pound 11 ounces) sauerkraut
1 tablespoon dried dill weed
Butter, salt, and ground black pepper

In a kettle, combine sausages, potatoes, dill seed, salt
and enough water to generously cover. Cover and heat to
boiling. Remove sausages when heated through but not
split (about 10 minutes); keep warm. Continue cooking
potatoes until just tender; drain. Meantime, in another
pan, simmer sauerkraut in its own juices with dill weed
until heated through. Serve sausage, potato and sauerkraut to each person. Pass butter, salt and pepper for
potato.

Maryland Scrapple   **6 servings**

This recipe is just for preparing the scrapple mixture. Once in camp, you cut it into ½-inch-thick slices, and fry them in a generous amount of shortening until crisp and brown. Serve scrapple for breakfast or supper with maple syrup or spiced applesauce over the top. For snow-camping or regular camping, you can prepare the scrapple mixture at home, pour it into washed cardboard milk cartons, chill, and freeze it. In camp, slice and fry.

1 quart boiling water
1 cup white corn meal
About ½ teaspoon salt
¼ teaspoon *each* crumbled dried thyme, savory, and sage or marjoram
1 pound bulk pork sausage or finely chopped smoked ham

Stirring constantly, gradually add boiling water to corn meal in top part of double boiler. Stir in remaining ingredients. Place over simmering water, and cook, uncovered, for 1½ hours, stirring frequently. Correct seasoning. Pour into bread loaf pans (9 by 5 inches) or other long, narrow pans. Cool.

Liver Pâté

You make this at home, then carry it to camp to slice for sandwiches or spread on crackers.

2 pounds lean boneless pork, cubed
1 clove garlic, peeled
Salted water
3 pounds calf liver
1 onion, sliced
2 bay leaves
6 whole cloves
½ teaspoon sugar
About ½ teaspoon salt
About 1 teaspoon mace
Black pepper

Cook pork and garlic in salted water to cover until pork is very tender. Drain, saving 2 cups of the liquid. Combine the reserved liquid, liver, onion, bay, cloves, sugar, and salt; and cook until liver is very tender. Add cooked pork. Chill for 8 hours. Force pork and liver through food grinder fitted with a fine blade. Season mixture to taste with mace, salt, and pepper. Press into a bread loaf pan (9 by 5 inches). Bake in a moderate oven (350°) for 20 minutes. Cool, remove fat, and wrap until use.

Paella Valenciana

6 servings

1 frying chicken (2½ to 3 pounds), cut into serving
    pieces
4 to 8 link pork sausages
1/3 cup olive oil
1 cup long-grain white rice
1 clove garlic, minced or mashed
½ bay leaf
About 1½ teaspoons salt (to taste)
½ teaspoon ground black pepper
Pinch of saffron (or use turmeric)
2 cups boiling water
1 pound mixed fresh or canned shelled shellfish (oysters,
    clams, shrimp)
1 can (1 pound) peas, drained
1 large can or jar (4 ounces) sliced pimentos

In a deep frying pan or Dutch oven, brown chicken and
sausage well in olive oil. Stir in rice, garlic, bay, salt,
pepper, and saffron. Cover and cook over medium heat
for 5 minutes. Add water, shellfish, peas, and pimentos.
Cover and cook over low heat until rice is tender, about
25 minutes; gently stir frequently during cooking.

Paella, Trail Version   6 to 8 servings

4½ quarts water
Salt
¼ pound butter or margarine
2 ounces dried mushrooms
1 ounce dehydrated green pepper flakes
¾ pound (about 4 cups) packaged precooked (instant) rice
4 ounces freeze-dried tuna
4 ounces freeze-dried prawns (or dried shrimp)
1 teaspoon *each* dill weed, crumbled dried rosemary, and
    turmeric
½ teaspoon garlic powder
Ground black pepper
1 can (7 ounces) tuna packed in oil

Put water, 1½ teaspoons salt, and butter into a kettle;
heat to boiling. Add mushrooms and pepper flakes. Boil
for 10 minutes. Add rice, freeze-dried tuna, prawns, dill,
rosemary, turmeric, garlic powder, and about ½ teaspoon black pepper. Cover, and simmer until tuna and
prawns are reconstituted, about 5 minutes. Stir in
canned tuna with oil. Taste and correct seasoning.
Remove from heat, cover and let stand for about 5
minutes to allow rice and meats to absorb all liquid and
seasonings to blend.

Chicken and Rice

1 chicken (about 3 pounds), cut into serving pieces
1 cup long-grain white rice
1 medium-sized onion, finely chopped
1 stalk celery, finely chopped
¼ pound fresh mushrooms, thinly sliced
1 teaspoon salt
½ teaspoon ground black pepper
2½ cups water (or use half water and half dry white
    table wine)

Combine all ingredients in a heavy kettle or Dutch oven.
Cover, heat to boiling, then simmer for 30 minutes or
until chicken is tender.

Variation: For a quicker version, prepare as above *except* substitute about 4 small cans (5 ounces *each*)
canned chicken for fresh. Substitute 1½ cups packaged
precooked (instant) rice for long-grain. Simmer for only
about 15 minutes.

Chicken and Rice, Trail Version   6 to 8 servings

8 ounces freeze-dried chicken
2 ounces dehydrated onion flakes
2 ounces dehydrated celery flakes
1 ounce dried mushrooms
3 cups water (or, better, use half water and half dry
    white table wine)
1 teaspoon salt
1 teaspoon ground black pepper
1 tablespoon crumbled dried tarragon
2 chicken bouillon cubes
1 tablespoon butter
8 ounces (about 2½ cups) packaged precooked (instant)
    rice

In a large kettle, combine chicken, onions, celery, mushrooms, and 2 cups of the water; let stand for 10 to 15
minutes. Stir in salt, pepper, tarragon, bouillon cubes,
and butter. Cover, heat to boiling, then simmer for 15
minutes or until ingredients are tender and blended. Add
rice and remaining water. Cover, heat to boiling, then
remove from heat and let stand for 10 minutes or until
rice is tender.

Fried Chicken and Gravy 6 servings

Serve with corn bread or rice or potatoes.

2 small frying chickens (about 2½ pounds *each*), cut into
    serving pieces
2 tablespoons flour
1 teaspoon paprika
Salt
Ground black pepper
About ¼ cup cooking oil
1 cup milk
1 tablespoon sherry (optional)

Combine flour, paprika, 1½ teaspoons salt, and about ¾
teaspoon pepper in a clean paper bag. Add chicken, and
shake to coat with flour mixture. In a large frying pan or
Dutch oven, over medium-high heat, brown chicken
pieces well on all sides in oil. Reduce heat, cover, and
cook for about 20 minutes more or until tender. Drain
chicken on paper toweling. Meantime, add remaining
flour and seasonings to drippings in frying pan. Stir until
slightly browned and a smooth paste. Gradually add
milk, cooking and stirring over low heat to make a
smooth and thickened sauce. Season to taste with salt
and pepper. Stir in sherry.

Chicken and Dumplings*　　　　　　　　**6 to 7 servings**

Good accompaniments: green salad and white table wine.

1 roasting chicken (about 6 pounds), cut into serving
　　pieces
2 tablespoons crumbled dried tarragon
1 teaspoon salt
1 teaspoon ground black pepper
Water
Dumpling dough (page 148) or 1 package (10) refrigera-
　　tor biscuits
Paprika

Remove fat from chicken cavity at back and rib areas. Finely chop fat. Place fat, chicken, tarragon, salt, and pepper into a heavy kettle along with water about 3 inches deep in kettle. Heat to boiling, then cover and simmer for 40 minutes or until chicken is almost tender. Drop dumpling dough onto bubbling stew. Or cut each biscuit in half, and arrange pieces over top of stew. Sprinkle dumplings generously with paprika. Cover tightly and simmer for 20 minutes or until dumplings are done. (Break open one test dumpling to check for doneness; biscuit dumplings will resemble soft bread.)

*See *Food for Knapsackers* for a trail version of this dish.

Chicken Gumbo

Good accompaniments: lettuce wedges with oil and vinegar dressing, and poppy seed rolls.

4 pounds frying chicken pieces
2 tablespoons butter or olive oil
1 clove garlic, minced or mashed
1 can (1 pound) small boiling onions, drained
1 can (1 pound) tomatoes (stewed, wedges, or peeled whole)
1 pound fresh or frozen okras
1 whole lemon, very thinly sliced
1 teaspoon *each* salt, ground black pepper, and crumbled dried basil

Combine all ingredients in a Dutch oven or heavy kettle, cover, and simmer for about 1 hour or until chicken is tender.

Wild Duck Roast

To cook more ducks and serve more people, simply mutiply the recipe accordingly. Serve duck with wild rice, brown rice, or Rice for Ducks (page 113).

1 wild duck, cleaned and plucked
Salt
Garlic powder (optional)
1 medium-sized onion
1 stalk celery
1 tablespoon flour
¾ cup dry white table wine or water

Wash duck, dry well, and rub inside and out with salt and garlic powder. Insert onion and celery in duck cavity. Place duck in a Dutch oven, cover, bury in coals, and cook about 1 hour. Remove duck and keep warm. To make gravy: Remove celery and onion from duck cavity, chop finely, and return to juices in Dutch oven. Sprinkle with flour, and stir to make a smooth paste. Gradually add wine, and cook and stir until smooth and thick. Add salt to taste. Serve gravy with duck.

Fried Rabbit with Gravy 5 to 6 servings

1 rabbit (3½ to 4 pounds), cut into serving pieces
4 tablespoons flour
1 tablespoon salt
½ teaspoon ground black pepper
½ teaspoon garlic powder
6 to 8 tablespoons cooking oil
1 cup milk (or dry white table wine or beer)

Combine flour, salt, pepper, and garlic powder in a clean paper bag. Add rabbit, and shake to coat with flour mixture. In a large frying pan, heat oil at medium-high heat. Add rabbit pieces, and brown on one side. Turn pieces, cover pan, place over a lower fire, and cook for 25 minutes more or until rabbit is tender. Remove rabbit from pan and keep warm. To make gravy: Add remaining seasoned flour to pan, and stir to make a smooth paste. Gradually add milk, and cook and stir until smooth and thick. Correct seasoning.

Rabbit Borracho   **4 servings**

Good accompaniments: green salad, buttered noodles
sprinkled with grated Parmesan cheese, and fruit and
cheese.

1 rabbit (3½ pounds), cut into serving pieces
4 to 5 cups dry red table wine
24 Chinese parsley leaves*
1 sprig fresh oregano or 1 tablespoon crumbled dried
    oregano
1 teaspoon *each* salt, cayenne, and garlic powder
½ cup water
1/3 cup flour

Put rabbit into a large bowl. Combine remaining ingredients except flour and water; and pour over rabbit. Cover,
chill, and let marinate for 24 hours; turn occasionally.
Put rabbit with marinade into a heavy kettle. Cover and
simmer for about 1 hour or until meat is tender. Remove
meat. Gradually stir water into flour to make a smooth
paste. Gradually add about half of the paste to stew
juices, stirring. Cook for about 5 minutes more, stirring
occasionally, until sauce is smooth and thickened. (Add
more of the paste if you wish a thicker sauce.) Return
meat to kettle and heat through.

*Also known as *cilantro* (in Mexican and Spanish markets) or
coentro (in Portuguese markets). If you cannot get it, you can
substitute regular parsley; but the flavor effect will not be so
exotic.

Fish Baked in the Coals 6 or more

To make this recipe, you will need cloths, seaweed, newspapers, and a hot fire built upon sand.

1 large whole salmon or other fish (about 5 or 6
     pounds), cleaned
2 tablespoons salt
1 tablespoon ground black pepper
2 cloves garlic, slivered, or 1 tablespoon garlic powder
2 bay leaves

Rub fish surfaces with salt and pepper. With a sharp knife, pierce flesh in several places, and insert garlic sliver in each (or rub fish with garlic powder). Wrap fish and bay leaves with one layer of damp cloths, then in a layer of seaweed, then in a layer of damp newspaper three more times. Push the cooking fire aside. Dig a bed in the hot sand, about the same size and shape as fish packet. Put a thick layer of fire coals over the bottom of the bed. Put in the fish packet. Cover with more hot coals, then with sand. Allow fish to cook for about 20 minutes per pound. Uncover, unwrap, and lift fish from bones to serve.

Fried Catfish

Just as soon as possible after catching, clean all fish, prepare them for cooking, and keep them cool. If the catcher and the cook are not the same person, be sure to determine ahead of time who is responsible for cleaning the fish, so that there will be no time delay. You can use this cooking method for any small whole fish.

1 cleaned small whole catfish
¼ cup white or yellow corn meal
1 teaspoon salt
½ teaspoon ground black pepper
4 to 5 tablespoons bacon drippings

Combine corn meal, salt, and pepper in a plastic or paper bag, add fish, and shake to coat. Heat bacon drippings over high heat in a heavy frying pan. Add fish, and fry, turning once or twice, until it is golden brown and flakes easily with a fork.

Golden (Bob) Rules for Preparing Trout

1. Keep caught trout cool while fishing by packing them in moist grass in a creel as soon as they are caught. Clean the fish promptly. Do not carry them in plastic bags because the fish are likely to get too warm; then their fats turn to oils, and the flesh can take on a fishy odor and taste.

2. The best preparation for trout less than 12 inches long is frying or poaching. The best preparation for larger trout is baking or broiling, then filleting (boning).

3. Butter, margarine, or salad oil is preferable to bacon drippings for frying because the strong flavor of bacon can overpower fresh trout's delicate flavor.

4. A test for doneness in cooking: the fish flesh should flake when lifted with a fork, and should fall away readily from the bones.

5. To bone cooked trout, use a thin-bladed, sharp knife. Cut through the flesh from the tail, along the back, to just behind the head. Cut the flesh from the bone by running your knife, flat, along the backbone and over the rib bones.

6. Cold fried trout are delicious the following day for lunch — in camp or on the trail. To store overnight, cool it, and wrap it in waxed paper.

7. To season trout when cooking it for breakfast or lunch, use only salt and pepper. To season it for dinner, you can extend the seasoning with lemon juice, white wine, basil, or parsley.

Golden (Bob) Trout Parmesan

2 servings

2 tablespoons butter
2 tablespoons flour
About ¾ teaspoon salt
Water
¼ cup grated or shredded Parmesan cheese
2 medium-sized trout (about ½ pound *each*), dressed
¼ teaspoon ground black pepper
Juice of 1 lemon
2 tablespoons dehydrated parsley flakes

To make sauce: Melt butter in a saucepan. Stir in flour and ¼ teaspoon of the salt to make a paste. Gradually add 1 cup hot water, cooking and stirring over medium heat to make a smooth, thickened sauce. Simmer for 1 to 2 minutes, and stir in Parmesan. Keep sauce warm. Put trout in a shallow pan, add ½ teaspoon salt, pepper, lemon juice, parsley, and enough boiling water to cover. Simmer until fish flakes. Remove fish from water, bone, and serve the fillets topped with the Parmesan sauce.

Broiled Salmon Steaks 4 servings

This same preparation works well for other large-fish steaks or fillets such as mahimahi, halibut, or bass.

4 salmon steaks, ½ pound *each*
1 cup soy sauce
1 tablespoon dry mustard

Stir together soy and mustard. Pour over fish, and let marinate for 1 hour; turn fish occasionally. Place steaks on oiled grill, and broil over moderately hot charcoal, just until fish flakes with a fork. Do not allow fish to become dry. Or grill steaks on a lightly oiled grill or in a lightly oiled frying pan set over a medium-high open fire.

Variation: Cut fish into 1½-inch cubes, marinate in soy-mustard sauce as above. Thread fish cubes onto skewers, alternating with whole cherry tomatoes or large tomato wedges and 1½-inch cucumber chunks. Baste with oil, and broil over open fire until fish barely flakes.

Salmon Gumbo   6 servings

Good accompaniments: crisp cabbage slaw and cold beer.

3 pounds boneless salmon, cut into 1-inch chunks
4 medium-sized onions, finely chopped
1 small green bell pepper, finely chopped
4 or 5 celery stalks, finely chopped
3 tablespoons canned tomato paste
1 can (about 8 ounces) tomatoes (stewed, wedges, or
    peeled whole)
1 whole small lemon, thinly sliced
2 cloves garlic, minced or mashed
1 bay leaf
1 tablespoon salt
1 tablespoon gumbo filé powder*
Generous dash of Tabasco sauce
Hot steamed rice

Combine all ingredients except rice in a large kettle. Cover and simmer for about 15 minutes or just until salmon flakes with a fork. Serve over rice.

Variations: 1) Substitute any other large fish such as halibut, perch, bass, or rockfish. 2) Substitute about 4 cans (about 8 ounces *each*) canned salmon, drained, for fresh salmon. Follow directions above *except* do not add salmon until after vegetables have simmered; then add salmon and just heat through.

*Pulverized sassafras leaves

Curried Fish Steaks

4 steaks or fillets of salmon, mahimahi, bass, or other
    large fish, about ½ pound *each*
1 medium-sized onion, thinly sliced
1 teaspoon grated fresh ginger root (or about ¼ teaspoon
    ground ginger)
2 to 3 tablespoons salad oil
4 cloves garlic, minced or mashed
1 teaspoon curry powder
¼ teaspoon salt
2 cups white wine vinegar

In a frying pan or saucepan, sauté onion and fresh ginger
in oil for about 3 minutes. Stir in garlic, curry, salt, and
vinegar (and ground ginger if used), and heat to boiling.
Place fish pieces in a bowl. Pour curry mixture over fish,
and allow fish to marinate for 5 or 6 hours; keep fish
cool, and turn occasionally. Place fish on greased rack
set over medium coals, and broil until it flakes; turn
once.

Variation: Marinate 1½-inch cubes of fish instead of
steaks or fillets. Thread on skewers, alternating with
mushroom caps and cherry tomatoes. Broil.

Ginger Fish

About 3 pounds fish steaks (firm-fleshed white fish such
   as swordfish, halibut, rockfish); *or* about 2 pounds
   large fish, cut into about 1½-inch chunks along with
   your choice of accompanying vegetables: mushrooms,
   cherry tomatoes, eggplant chunks, and/or zucchini
   chunks
1 medium-sized onion, finely chopped
1 teaspoon minced fresh ginger root or about ½ teaspoon dried ginger
2 tablespoons salad oil
3 to 4 cloves garlic
1 teaspoon curry powder
¼ teaspoon salt
2 cups vinegar

Sauté onion and ginger in oil until onions are limp. Stir
in garlic, curry, salt, and vinegar; heat to boiling. Pour
over fish steaks or fish and vegetable chunks. Cover and
chill for 24 hours, turning occasionally. Pan-broil fish
steaks; thread fish chunks and vegetables onto skewers,
and broil over open fire.

Mahimahi Steaks   4 servings

Good accompaniments: hot rice and a cold green salad.

4 mahimahi steaks, each about ½ pound
1 cup soy sauce
About ¼ cup butter

Place fish in a bowl, pour soy over, and allow to marinate for about 2 hours; keep fish cool, and turn occasionally. Drain fish. Melt butter in a large frying pan over
medium-high heat. Add fish, and lightly brown on one
side, turn and cook on second side just until fish flakes.

Variation: Drain marinated fish and place on greased
grill or rack set over open fire. Grill or broil just until
fish flakes. Turn fish once. Baste frequently with a
mixture of about equal parts melted butter and soy.

Tuna Chowder   6 servings

1 can (10½ ounces) condensed cream of celery soup
1 onion, finely chopped
1 stalk celery, finely diced
6 cups water
1 tablespoon chopped fresh parsley
1 teaspoon salt
½ teaspoon paprika
1 can (about 12 ounces) tuna with oil
1 to 2 tablespoons sherry

Combine all ingredients except tuna and sherry in a
kettle; cover and simmer for about 10 minutes, or until
celery is just tender. Add tuna, and simmer for about 5
minutes more. Stir in sherry.

Creamed Tuna with Ginger over Noodles   6 servings

Good accompaniments: lettuce wedges with French dressing or sliced tomatoes sprinkled with lemon juice and tarragon or basil.

6 tablespoons butter
1/3 cup flour
3 cups milk
3 tablespoons grated or slivered fresh ginger root (or about 2 teaspoons ground ginger)
½ pound fresh mushrooms, thinly sliced or 1 can (6 ounces) sliced mushrooms, drained
3 cans (about 8 ounces *each*) tuna, drained
1 teaspoon salt
¼ teaspoon ground black pepper
12 ounces egg noodles (red or green, if available), cooked *al dente* and drained

In a large saucepan or kettle, melt butter. Stir in flour to make a smooth paste. Gradually add milk, cooking and stirring over low heat to make a smooth and thickened sauce. Stir in ginger, mushrooms, tuna, salt, and pepper. Simmer until heated through. Serve over noodles.

Variation: Substitute 6 ounces freeze-dried tuna for canned and ½ ounce dried mushrooms, broken into bits, for fresh. Soak tuna and mushrooms in water to just cover. Then proceed as directed above.

Lamarou

1 pound skinned and boned dried salted cod
Water
2 pounds potatoes, peeled and cut into 1-inch cubes
2 tablespoons olive oil
2 cloves garlic, minced or mashed
1 teaspoon dill seed
½ teaspoon ground black pepper
¾ cup chopped fresh parsley or 3 tablespoons dehydrated parsley flakes
1 tablespoon crumbled dried thyme
1 tablespoon crumbled dried basil

Soak cod in cold water until it is very moist throughout, about 12 to 24 hours; change water 2 or 3 times. (Or freshen cod according to package directions.) Drain. Break into bite-sized pieces, and combine in a kettle with potatoes, oil, garlic, dill, and pepper. Cover and simmer for about 30 minutes or until potatoes and fish are tender. Add parsley, thyme, and basil, and simmer for a few minutes more.

Variation: For trail version, prepare as above *except* use 12 ounces dehydrated potato dices instead of fresh potatoes and use 3 tablespoons dehydrated parsley flakes instead of fresh parsley.

Headhunter Fried Rice

1 pound raw shrimp or canned shrimp
Boiling salted water
4 tablespoons cooking oil
1 large onion, finely chopped
1 cup sliced fresh or canned mushrooms
2 cups finely chopped chard
1 cup Chinese sugar peas in pods (optional)
2 tablespoons finely chopped green bell peppers
2 tablespoons finely chopped sweet red peppers
1 teaspoon minced or grated fresh ginger root (or about
    ½ teaspoon ground ginger)
About ¼ teaspoon crushed dried hot red pepper
¼ pound cooked chicken or turkey, finely chopped
¼ pound cooked ham or pork, finely chopped
3 cups cooked rice
About 1 teaspoon salt
3 to 4 tablespoons chopped Chinese parsley (optional)
Soy sauce

Drop shrimp into boiling salted water and cook just until
they turn pink, drain, and peel; drain canned shrimp. In
a large frying pan, sauté onion in cooking oil until
golden. Add mushrooms, chard, sugar peas, green and
red peppers, ginger and hot pepper, chicken, ham, and
all shrimp. Cook and stir over high heat until vegetables
are hot. Add rice and salt to season, mix in well, and
sauté over high heat until vegetables are tender-crisp and
rice is heated through, about 10 minutes. Stir in Chinese
parsley. Pass soy sauce.

Headhunter Fried Rice, Trail Style

6 servings

6 ounces freeze-dried or dried oriental shrimp
6 ounces freeze-dried chicken or turkey
6 ounces freeze-dried ham or pork
2 ounces dried mushrooms
1 cup dehydrated spinach flakes
1 tablespoon dehydrated onion flakes
1 tablespoon dehydrated sweet green pepper flakes
1 tablespoon dehydrated sweet red pepper flakes
About ¼ teaspoon crushed dried hot red pepper
Water
10 ounces (about 3¼ cups) packaged precooked
     (instant) rice
4 tablespoons cooking oil
1 teaspoon minced or grated fresh ginger root (or about
     ½ teaspoon ground ginger)
About 1 teaspoon salt
Soy sauce

Combine shrimp, chicken, ham, mushrooms, spinach flakes, onion flakes, green and red pepper flakes, and hot pepper; add water to just cover; and allow to stand until soft. Drain off water, and save 3½ cups. Heat water to boiling, add rice, remove from heat, cover, and let stand for 10 minutes. In a large frying pan over medium-high heat, sauté drained meats and vegetables in oil for about 5 minutes. Add rice, ginger, and salt to season; sauté until heated through, about 10 minutes. Pass soy sauce.

Eggs and Cheese

A few suggestions for making egg dishes more inter-
esting:

1. Omelets: Add crumbled smoked cheese, or snipped
   chives, or chopped anchovies to the mixture. Or put a
   teaspoon of caviar and a teaspoon of sour cream in
   the center of the omelet before folding it.
2. Scrambled eggs: Add finely chopped smoked or kip-
   pered meats or fish.
3. Fried or scrambled eggs: Put a drop or two of herb
   vinegar into the butter.
4. Fried eggs: Add a little milk to the butter, cover, and
   slowly simmer.

Scrambled Eggs with Basil   6 servings

1 dozen eggs
1 teaspoon lemon juice
1 teaspoon snipped fresh basil or about ½ teaspoon
   crumbled dried basil
About ½ teaspoon salt
3 tablespoons butter

Beat eggs with lemon juice, basil, and salt. In a large,
heavy frying pan, over medium-high heat, melt the
butter. Add eggs, and gently stir and lift just until set
but moist.

Variation: For the trail, follow directions above except
substitute 6 ounces powdered eggs, which have been
mixed with water or milk to make a medium-thick
batter, for the fresh eggs.

Scrambled Eggs with Chorizo

6 servings

¼ pound chorizo (spicy Mexican or Portuguese sausages), cut from casings and crumbled
1 dozen eggs
1 teaspoon lemon juice
1 tablespoon chopped fresh parsley
About ½ teaspoon salt
Butter or cooking oil

In a large, heavy frying pan, over medium heat, lightly brown sausage. Add butter or cooking oil, if necessary, to make about 3 tablespoons drippings in frying pan. Increase heat to medium-high. Beat eggs with lemon juice, parsley and salt. Add eggs to pan, and gently stir and lift just until set but still moist.

Variation: For the trail, follow directions above except substitute 6 ounces powdered eggs, which have been mixed with water or milk to make a medium-thick batter, for the fresh eggs.

Scrambled Eggs with Herbs

6 servings

1 dozen eggs
1 teaspoon lemon juice
1 tablespoon crumbled dried thyme, tarragon, or savory
About ½ teaspoon salt
3 tablespoons butter

Beat eggs with lemon juice, thyme, and salt. In a large, heavy frying pan, melt butter over medium-high heat. Add eggs, and gently stir and lift just until set but still moist.

Variation: For the trail, follow directions above except substitute 6 ounces powdered eggs, which have been mixed with water or milk to make a medium-thick batter, for the fresh eggs.

Scrambled Eggs with Tomatoes   **6 servings**

1 dozen eggs
2 medium-sized tomatoes, peeled and chopped
3 tablespoons olive oil
1 tablespoon snipped fresh tarragon leaves or about 1
    teaspoon crumbled dried tarragon
About ½ teaspoon salt

In a large heavy frying pan, sauté tomatoes in olive oil, over low heat, until tender. Beat eggs with tarragon and salt. Increase heat to medium-high. Add eggs to pan, and gently stir and lift just until set but still moist.

Variation: Follow directions above except substitute 6 ounces powdered eggs, which have been mixed with water or tomato juice to make a medium-thick batter, for the fresh eggs. If necessary, substitute 2 peeled whole canned tomatoes for the fresh.

Brains and Eggs   **5 to 6 servings**

1 calf brain (2 sections) or 2 lamb brains (4 sections)
4 tablespoons butter
6 eggs
1 tablespoon chopped fresh parsley
Dash of Tabasco sauce
Salt and ground black pepper

Wash brains well in cool water. Remove membrane. Chop brains. Heat butter until bubbling in a large frying pan. Add brains, and cook, stirring until just set. Beat eggs with parsley, Tabasco, and salt and pepper to season. Add to frying pan, and cook slowly, stirring until set but still moist, as for scrambled eggs.

Variation: Substitute 1 teaspoon grated fresh ginger root for Tabasco.

Huevos Rancheros (Ranch Eggs)　　　　　　6 servings

1 dozen eggs
½ pound bacon slices, cut into about 1-inch pieces
1 large can (about 1 pound, 13 ounces) tomatoes with
　　juices, chopped; or 1 small can (6 ounces) tomato
　　paste mixed with 1½ cans water
2 2-inch canned *jalapenos* (very hot green peppers),
　　finely chopped, or about ¾ teaspoon crushed dried
　　hot red peppers
2 large cloves garlic, very thinly sliced
About ¼ teaspoon salt
6 slices toast

In a large frying pan, over low heat, cook bacon until
almost crisp. Stir in tomatoes, *jalapenos*, garlic and salt.
Simmer, covered, stirring occasionally, until blended and
thickened to a sauce. Break eggs into sauce, cover, and
allow to poach until set, about 3 to 5 minutes. Lift 2
eggs onto each toast slice, and top and surround with
sauce. (If necessary, poach only part of the eggs at one
time.)

Mushroom Omelet   1 serving

1½ to 2 ounces mushrooms, thinly sliced
1 tablespoon butter
Few drops of fresh lemon juice
2 eggs
Salt and pepper to taste

In a medium-sized frying pan, sauté mushrooms in about
half of the butter until tender; remove from pan. Add
remaining butter to pan, and place over medium-high
heat until it bubbles. Beat eggs with lemon juice, salt,
and pepper. Pour into pan, and tilt pan and lift eggs at
edges to allow uncooked portion of egg to flow to
bottom of pan. When eggs are partially set, sprinkle
mushrooms over one half. Fold second half over mushrooms. Heat through, and slip onto serving plate.

Sausage Omelet   1 serving

4 tablespoons chopped sausages or salami or lunch meat
About 1 tablespoon butter
2 eggs
1 teaspoon lemon juice
Salt and pepper to taste

In a medium-sized frying pan, brown sausages in half of
the butter; remove from pan. Add remaining butter to
pan, and heat over medium-high heat until it bubbles.
Beat eggs with lemon juice, salt, and pepper. Pour into
pan, and tilt pan and lift eggs at edges to allow uncooked
portion of egg to flow to bottom of pan. When eggs are
partially set, sprinkle sausages over one half. Fold second
half over sausages. Heat through, and slip onto serving
plate.

Cheese Omelet 1 serving

2 eggs
½ teaspoon chopped fresh parsley
Salt and pepper to taste
1 tablespoon butter
2 tablespoons finely chopped or shredded natural cheese
   such as Cheddar, Swiss, or blue

Beat eggs with parsley, salt, and pepper. In a medium-sized frying pan, heat butter over medium-high heat, until it bubbles. Pour in eggs, and tilt pan and lift eggs at edges to allow uncooked portion of egg to flow to bottom of pan. When eggs are partially set, sprinkle cheese over one half. Fold second half over the cheese. Heat through, and slip onto serving plate.

Deviled Eggs, Curried 6 servings

To package deviled eggs for carrying, wrap each one in waxed paper and twist the paper ends.

1 dozen hard-cooked eggs, sliced in half lengthwise
2 tablespoons mayonnaise
2 teaspoons curry powder
1 tablespoon dry mustard
½ teaspoon *each* salt, cayenne, and ground coriander

Lift yolks from eggs, mash well with a fork, add remaining ingredients except egg whites, and stir and mash together to make a smooth paste. Fill egg white cavities with the yolk mixture. Press two egg halves together.

Variation: Hot Curried Eggs: Wrap each hard-cooked egg in a thin slice of boiled ham, and arrange in a single layer in a shallow baking dish. Stir 1 teaspoon curry powder into 1 cup Medium Cream Sauce (page 152). Spoon sauce over eggs. Slip under broiler until sauce lightly browns.

Pimento Cheese Spread

Use this as a sandwich spread. It is especially good for toasted or grilled sandwiches. For fullest flavor, make the spread ahead of time so that it can chill for several hours.

1 pound natural Cheddar, Monterey Jack, or longhorn cheese (or a mixture of two or three cheeses), shredded
1 small can (2 ounces) pimentos, finely chopped
1 tablespoon finely grated onion
1 tablespoon caraway seed
1 tablespoon dry mustard
1 teaspoon fresh lemon juice
½ teaspoon salt
About ¼ teaspoon black pepper
About 3 tablespoons mayonnaise

Stir all ingredients together to mix well. Add a little more mayonnaise if necessary to make a medium-thick spread.

Potatoes, Rice, Dry Beans, Grains

Potatoes with Cheese   6 servings

3 large potatoes, peeled and cut into 1/8-inch-thick
    crosswise slices
Boiling salted water
2 large onions, thinly sliced
1 teaspoon salt
About 1 teaspoon black pepper
1 tablespoon butter
¼ pound sharp Cheddar cheese, shredded

Cook potatoes, covered, in boiling salted water for 10
minutes; drain. Arrange half of the potatoes over bottom
of a buttered heavy frying pan or kettle. Top with half
of the onions, sprinkle with half of the salt and pepper,
dot with half of the butter, and sprinkle with half of the
cheese. Repeat layering to use all ingredients. Cover and
cook over low heat until potatoes and onions are tender,
about 30 minutes.

Shallow-Fried Sweet Potatoes   6 servings

2 pounds sweet potatoes, peeled, and cut crosswise into
    ½-inch-thick slices
Cooking oil
Salt

Heat ½ inch oil in bottom of a deep frying pan to
medium-hot. Add potato slices, a few at a time, and fry
until crisp on the outside and soft inside. Drain on paper
towels. Sprinkle with salt, and serve hot.

Instant Creamy Potatoes   6 servings

10 ounces instant mashed potato powder
Boiling salted water
1½ ounces packaged powdered sour cream sauce
1 cup milk
1 tablespoon snipped chives
1 tablespoon butter
1 teaspoon salt
About ½ teaspoon black pepper

Prepare mashed potatoes with boiling salted water according to package directions. Stir in remaining ingredients, and beat until smooth and fluffy. If mixture is
not fluffy enough, add more milk. Stir mixture over low
heat until it is steaming hot.

Whipped Sweet Potatoes   6 servings

2 pounds sweet potatoes, peeled and cut into 1- to
    2-inch chunks
Boiling salted water
3 tablespoons butter
About 1 teaspoon salt
2 eggs
1 cup milk
3 tablespoons honey
1 teaspoon ground cinnamon
1 teaspoon ground nutmeg

Cook potatoes, covered, in boiling salted water until
soft. Drain off all but about 3 tablespoons water. Mash
potatoes well with remaining water. Add butter and salt
to taste. Beat eggs lightly; beat in milk, honey, cinnamon, and nutmeg; gradually add to potatoes, beating
until well mixed. Serve while hot.

Stewed Sweet Potatoes   **6 servings**

2 pounds sweet potatoes, peeled and cut into ½-inch-
    thick crosswise slices
½ cup brown sugar, firmly packed
1 tablespoon flour
2 tablespoons ground cinnamon
1 teaspoon salt
½ cup water
3 tablespoons butter

Spread half of the potatoes over bottom of a Dutch oven
or heavy frying pan. Stir together sugar, flour, cinnamon, salt, and water; pour half of the mixture over
potatoes. Dot with half of the butter. Top with a layer
of remaining potatoes, top with remaining sugar mixture; dot with remaining butter. Cover tightly, and cook
over low heat until potatoes are tender, about 15 minutes (shake pan occasionally to prevent potatoes from
sticking to bottom).

Golden Rice   **6 servings**

Serve with curried meats, or alongside other meats or
vegetables.

10 ounces (about 3¼ cups) packaged precooked
    (instant) rice
3¼ cups water
1 teaspoon turmeric
About 1 teaspoon salt
1 tablespoon butter

In a kettle, heat water, turmeric, salt, and butter to
boiling. Stir in rice, cover, remove from heat, and let
stand for 10 minutes or until rice absorbs moisture and
is tender.

Rice for Ducks and Other Fowl   6 to 8 servings

This is really a stuffing recipe — enough for 2 ducks, chickens, or other small birds. But you can also make it up just as a rice dish to serve separately alongside ducks and other small fowl.

1 cup uncooked wild rice or brown rice
Water
¼ cup olive oil
½ cup finely chopped onions
½ cup finely chopped celery
¼ cup finely chopped green bell peppers
½ cup thinly sliced fresh mushrooms
1 tablespoon chopped fresh parsley
1 teaspoon salt
¼ cup sherry

Cover rice with warm water, and let stand for 30 minutes; drain, saving liquid. In a large kettle, lightly brown rice in olive oil. Add onions and celery, and sauté until limp. Add peppers and mushrooms, and sauté just until tender. Stir in parsley, salt, sherry, and reserved rice liquid. Cover tightly, and simmer for 40 minutes or until rice is tender.

Curried Rice and Potatoes   **6 servings**

5 ounces (about 1½ cups) packaged precooked (instant)
   rice
5 ounces dehydrated potato dices
4 tablespoons instant minced dried onions
3 tablespoons butter
About 1 teaspoon salt
About 1 teaspoon curry powder
Water

Combine potatoes, onions, butter, salt, curry powder,
and a generous amount of water in a large kettle. Cover
and gently boil until potatoes are tender. Drain and save
liquid; measure 2 cups, and return to ingredients in
kettle along with rice. Stir well. Cover, and heat to
boiling. Remove from heat, and let stand for 10 minutes
or until rice has absorbed the liquid and is tender.

Buckwheat Groats (for Dinner)   **4 servings**

1 pound groats
Water
1 bunch wild onions, chopped (optional)
About 4 tablespoons soy sauce

Heat and stir groats in a heavy frying pan until they are
toasted. Add enough water just to cover groats. Heat to
boiling. Remove from heat, cover, and let stand for 10
minutes or until the grain absorbs the water. Stir in
onions and soy to taste.

Beans with Cheese

Serve these beans as a side dish with Chili con Carne (page 55). Any beans left over after the meal are good reheated and served a second time. Merely add more cheese when you reheat.

1 pound dry pinto beans
6 cups water
1 teaspoon salt
¼ cup bacon drippings
1 teaspoon Tabasco sauce
½ cup shredded or diced sharp Cheddar cheese

Pour water over beans and let soak until skins are wrinkled — overnight or 4 hours. Add salt. Heat to boiling, then cover, and simmer for 3 to 4 hours or until beans are very tender. Drain off and save liquid from beans. Add bacon drippings and Tabasco to beans, mashing beans with a fork. Gradually add the reserved bean liquid, mixing and mashing until beans are a smooth, thick paste. Add cheese; and cook over low heat, stirring, until cheese melts. (Watch carefully to prevent sticking or burning. Add a little more liquid if mixture becomes too thick or sticky.)

Beans, Paul's Way

6 to 8 servings

1 pound dry pinto, red, or soy beans
Water
1 teaspoon salt
2 small hot dried peppers or about ½ teaspoon crumbled
    dried hot peppers (optional)
1 tablespoon crumbled dried basil
1 teaspoon ground sage
2 cloves garlic, minced or mashed
1 cup (about 4 ounces) shredded Cheddar or Monterey
    Jack cheese (optional)
1 cup alfalfa sprouts
½ cup chopped fresh parsley

Rinse beans. Place in a kettle, and add enough water to cover beans by about 2 inches. Cover and boil for 3 minutes, remove from heat, and allow to stand for 1 hour (or soak beans overnight). Heat to boiling, then simmer for 3 hours; add salt and hot peppers. Continue simmering for 30 minutes more; add basil, sage, and garlic. Simmer for 30 minutes more or until beans are tender and water is absorbed. Stir occasionally. (If necessary to keep beans moist during cooking, add a little water as needed.) Add cheese, and cook for 5 minutes more. Sprinkle each serving with alfalfa sprouts and parsley.

Variation: If you used pinto or red beans for this recipe, you can make any leftover beans into Refried Beans with Sprouts: Add enough water to leftover beans to moisten well. Slowly heat through, and mash. Spread onto flat bread or a crisp tortilla, sprinkle with a thick layer of shredded Cheddar or Monterey Jack cheese, and sprinkle with alfalfa sprouts.

116

Baked Lima Beans

6 servings

2 cups dry lima beans
2 quarts water
2 teaspoons salt
2 to 4 ounces bacon or salt pork, cut into about 1-inch
    strips
1 tablespoon brown sugar
2 teaspoons dry mustard
1 medium-sized onion, chopped
About ¼ teaspoon black pepper
1 cup (about ¼ pound) shredded sharp Cheddar cheese

Put beans into a kettle, add water, and let stand for 4 hours. Add 1 teaspoon of the salt, and the bacon, and simmer, covered, until tender, about 1 hour. Drain liquid from beans, saving 1½ cups. In camp: Combine beans, bean liquid, the remaining 1 teaspoon salt, the sugar, mustard, onion, pepper, and two-thirds of the cheese in a greased Dutch oven; sprinkle with remaining cheese; cover oven; bury in coals; and let cook for about 30 minutes. At home: Combine ingredients in a baking dish, and bake in a moderate oven (350°) until heated through, about 30 minutes.

New England Baked Beans

6 servings

2 cups small dry white beans
2 quarts water
2 teaspoons salt
¾ cup molasses
¾ cup catsup or chili sauce
1 tablespoon dry mustard
2 teaspoons Worcestershire
1 medium-sized onion, chopped
½ pound salt pork
1 cup strong black coffee

Put beans into a kettle, add water, and let stand overnight; or heat to boiling, then simmer, covered, for 30 minutes. Drain off and save liquid; stir in salt. In a baking dish, stir together 2 cups of the bean liquid, the molasses, catsup, mustard, Worcestershire, onion, and beans. Cut salt pork to, but not through, skin in ¼-inch slices; press into top of beans, cover, and bake in a slow oven (325°) for 2 hours. Check occasionally, and add a little more of the bean liquid as necessary to keep beans moist. Remove cover, pour coffee over beans, and bake for 1 hour longer.

Variation: To cook in the campfire: Follow directions above except soak and cook beans in a heavy kettle or Dutch oven. Cook over low campfire heat until beans are tender.

Vegetables

Some tips for fresher flavors:

Reconstitute freeze-dried items with some seasonings added to the water, rather than with water alone. For example, add some vinegar to the water used to reconstitute cabbage or salad vegetables. Add lemon juice to the water used to reconstitute peas, green beans, or other green vegetables.

Green Beans, Almonds, and Bacon 6 servings

1½ pounds fresh green beans, ends trimmed; or
    2 packages (10 ounces *each*) frozen beans; or
    2 cans (1 pound *each*) canned beans
Boiling salted water
4 tablespoons fresh lemon juice
4 tablespoons slivered almonds
3 slices bacon which have been cooked until crisp and
    crumbled

Cook fresh or frozen beans, uncovered, in boiling salted water until tender, and drain; or heat canned beans in their own juices, and drain. Toss with remaining ingredients, correct seasoning, and serve immediately.

Variation: For a trail version, soak 3 ounces freeze-dried beans in water to cover for about 10 minutes; then simmer until tender, about 5 minutes. Drain. Toss with seasonings as above.

Beets and Greens   **6 servings**

2 to 3 bunches young beets with greens
Boiling salted water
About 1 tablespoon butter
Salt and pepper
Fresh lemon juice or tarragon vinegar

Cut tops from beets, and trim off and discard stems
from the leafy green tops. Wash beets and greens well.
Cook beets only, covered, in enough boiling salted water
to cover until almost tender. Put greens over beets,
cover, and cook until beets and greens are tender, about
5 minutes. Drain. Peel and slice beets. Chop greens.
Keeping them separate, season beets and greens with
butter, salt, and pepper. To serve, arrange greens in a
mound, and surround with beet slices. Pass lemon juice
or tarragon vinegar.

Glazed Carrots   **6 servings**

6 to 8 carrots, sliced crosswise or cut into sticks
Boiling salted water
2 tablespoons butter
2 tablespoons honey
½ teaspoon caraway seed

Cook carrots, covered, in boiling salted water until
tender; drain. Melt butter; stir in honey and caraway
seed, and pour mixture over carrots. Turn to coat carrots
and heat through. Watch carefully to prevent burning.

Glazed Carrots and Apples

6 servings

6 to 8 carrots, thinly sliced crosswise
Boiling salted water
2 tablespoons butter
½ cup coarsely chopped unpeeled apples
2 tablespoons honey
½ teaspoon whole anise seeds

In a kettle, cook carrots, covered, in boiling salted water until tender; remove from kettle. Melt butter in kettle, add apples, and sauté just to coat with butter. Stir in honey and anise seed, then carrots. Cook over low heat, gently turning, just until mixture browns; do not let it burn.

Cabbage, Apples, and Cranberries

6 servings

Serve this dish with roasted chicken.

1½ pounds red cabbage, core removed and sliced very
    finely
3 slices bacon, cut into small pieces
1 cup fresh whole cranberries
2 unpeeled apples, cored and coarsely chopped
1 cup dry red table wine
¼ cup wine vinegar
½ cup brown sugar, loosely packed
1 teaspoon salt

In a large frying pan, cook bacon until crisp; remove and drain. Add cranberries, apples, wine, vinegar, sugar, and salt to frying pan. Cover, and simmer until cranberries pop. Add cabbage, cover, and simmer just until cabbage is barely tender, not limp, about 15 minutes. If necessary, add a little water. Sprinkle with bacon.

Herbed Celery Root 6 servings

1½ pounds celery root (celeriac), peeled and diced
½ cup water
½ cup milk
2 tablespoons snipped chives
½ teaspoon salt
About ¼ teaspoon black pepper
Dash of paprika
2 tablespoons chopped fresh parsley

Put celery root and water into a kettle, cover, heat to boiling, then simmer for about 10 minutes. Add remaining ingredients except parsley, and simmer, covered, for 5 minutes more or until celery root is tender. Sprinkle with parsley.

Spinach in Cream 6 servings

3 pounds fresh spinach, cooked, drained, and chopped;
    or 2 packages (about 10 ounces *each*) frozen chopped
    spinach, cooked and drained; or 1 large can (1 pound,
    11 ounces) spinach, heated in its own liquid, and
    drained
2 tablespoons butter
2 tablespoons flour
1 cup half-and-half (half milk and half cream)
½ teaspoon salt
About ½ teaspoon black pepper
¼ teaspoon ground nutmeg

Melt butter in a saucepan, and stir in flour to make a smooth paste. Gradually add half-and-half, and cook and stir to make a smooth and thickened sauce. Stir in salt, pepper, nutmeg, and spinach, and heat through.

Dandelion Greens   **6 servings**

Pick only young dandelion greens; the older ones are bitter.

2 to 3 pounds young tender dandelion greens
Boiling salted water
Lemon juice or vinegar or hot green chili pepper sauce

Cook greens, covered, in gently boiling water just until wilted and tender. Drain well. Season to taste with lemon juice, vinegar, or pepper sauce.

Turnips and Greens   **6 servings**

2 or 3 bunches young turnips with green tops
Boiling salted water
About 1 tablespoon butter
½ teaspoon salt
Black pepper
Fresh lemon juice or tarragon vinegar or hot green chili
    pepper sauce

Cut tops from turnips, and trim off and discard stems from leafy green tops. Wash greens well. Peel and slice turnips. Drop turnips into enough boiling salted water to cover. Cover with the greens; cover kettle, and gently boil for 15 minutes or until turnips are tender. Drain. Chop greens. Keeping them separate, season turnips and greens with butter, salt, and pepper. To serve, arrange greens in a mound, and surround with turnips. Pass lemon juice, tarragon vinegar, or pepper sauce.

Vegetables Roasted in Coals

Plan on 1 medium-sized baked potato per person and/or 1 ear of corn per person. Rub each potato with salad oil, and wrap in a wet newspaper. Leave corn in husks. Lay the vegetables around the edges of a good, hot bed of charcoal. Allow to roast until tender — about 1 hour for the potatoes, about 30 minutes for the corn; turn once or twice. Before serving, remove wrapping and brush ashes off the potatoes, and husk the corn. Serve with butter, salt, and pepper.

Guacamole   About 2 cups

Serve as an appetizer dip with crisp tortillas or crackers.

2 large ripe avocados, peeled and chopped
About ¼ teaspoon crushed dried hot red peppers
1 medium-sized onion, very finely chopped
1 medium-sized tomato, peeled, and chopped
1 clove garlic, minced or mashed
1 teaspoon fresh lemon juice
¾ teaspoon salt
About ½ teaspoon black pepper
Dash of Tabasco

Mash avocados with a fork. Add chili pepper, onion, tomato, and garlic, and mash together to blend. Stir in lemon juice, salt, pepper, and Tabasco. Correct seasoning.

Beet Salad   6 servings

Serve with fish or fowl or as a chilled salad alongside hot vegetables.

4 tablespoons olive oil
2 tablespoons fresh lemon juice
½ teaspoon dill weed
About ¼ teaspoon salt
2 cans (1 pound) sliced beets, drained; or 2 pounds fresh
    beets, cooked, peeled, and sliced

Shake or beat together oil, lemon juice, dill and salt to make a dressing; gently toss with beets. Chill.

Avocado Salad

6 servings

Serve on lettuce leaves, if you wish.

3 avocados, peeled and diced
4 tablespoons olive oil
4 tablespoons fresh lemon juice
½ teaspoon salt
¼ teaspoon pepper
About 6 large leaves of leaf lettuce (such as Australian,
    red, Boston [butter], or garden)
12 to 15 nasturtium leaves
1 cup coarsely chopped watercress sprigs

Shake or beat together oil, lemon juice, salt, and pepper
to make a dressing; gently toss with remaining ingredients.

Avocado Pineapple Salad

4 to 6 servings

This is good for lunch or dessert.

½ cup mayonnaise
2 tablespoons lemon juice
1 tablespoon sour cream
½ teaspoon salt
2 cups fresh pineapple chunks
Juice from pineapple
3 large ripe avocados, peeled and cut into large dices
2 stalks celery, chopped
1 large banana, sliced crosswise
12 walnut halves
Paprika

Stir together to make a dressing the mayonnaise, lemon
juice, sour cream, salt, and enough pineapple juice to
thin. Gently toss with remaining ingredients except
paprika. Sprinkle with paprika.

126

Papaya, Avocado and Grapefruit Salad   6 servings

3 papayas, peeled, seeded, and sliced lengthwise
2 ripe avocados, peeled and sliced lengthwise
2 grapefruits, peeled, and cut into sections, all white
    membrane removed
Crisp lettuce leaves
Salt
6 tablespoons lemon juice
4 tablespoons honey

Arrange papayas, avocados, and grapefruit on lettuce leaves on 6 salad plates. Sprinkle with salt. Beat lemon juice and honey together, and spoon over fruits.

Variation: Cut fruits into bite-sized chunks into a salad bowl, sprinkle with salt, and toss with combined lemon juice and honey. Serve from bowl or arrange on lettuce leaves.

Bean salad   6 to 8 servings

Serve bean salad on crisp lettuce leaves for lunch or as a meat accompaniment for dinner.

½ cup olive oil
¼ cup tarragon vinegar
½ teaspoon salt
1 small can (8 ounces) garbanzos (chickpeas), drained
1 small can (8 ounces) golden wax beans, drained
1 small can (8 ounces) kidney beans, drained
1 small can (8 ounces) green beans, drained
About ¼ teaspoon black pepper

Shake or beat together oil, vinegar, salt, and pepper to make a dressing; pour over beans, and mix thoroughly. Chill.

Kidney Bean Salad   6 servings

1 large can (1 pound, 11 ounces) kidney beans, drained
½ cup finely diced celery
¼ cup chopped green pepper
¼ cup chopped sweet pickles
3 hard-cooked eggs, diced or shredded
Salt
½ cup mayonnaise
1 tablespoon red wine vinegar
Crisp lettuce leaves
2 tomatoes, cut into slices or wedges

Combine beans, celery, green pepper, pickles, and eggs in
a salad bowl. Sprinkle with salt to season. Stir together
mayonnaise and vinegar; add to bowl, and toss to mix all
ingredients. Serve on crisp lettuce leaves. Garnish with
tomatoes.

White Bean Salad   6 servings

2 cups (about 1 pound) small dry white beans
Water
1 teaspoon *each* crumbled dried tarragon, salt, and
    ground black pepper
¼ cup oil-and-vinegar dressing
Lettuce leaves

Cover beans with water, boil for 2 minutes, remove from
heat, and let stand uncovered for 1 hour or more. Cover
beans and simmer until tender, about 2 hours; add more
water if necessary. Drain beans, mix with tarragon, salt,
and pepper; and chill. Before serving, toss with dressing.
Serve on lettuce.

Chinese Cabbage Salad   6 servings

Chinese cabbage is also called celery cabbage or *nappa*, or *won bok, wong nga bok*, or *siu choy*. Its compact, oblong, head is made up of wide stalks topped with leaves, and it is available in many supermarkets.

1½ pounds Chinese cabbage
1 large sweet onion
1/3 cup olive oil
¼ cup soy sauce
1 teaspoon crumbled dried oregano
½ teaspoon ground black pepper

Cut cabbage, diagonally across head, into thin slices. Very thinly slice onion crosswise, and break into rings. Put cabbage and onions into a bowl. Shake or beat together oil, soy, oregano, and pepper to make a dressing; pour over cabbage and onions. Toss lightly to mix.

Cabbage with Sour Cream   6 servings

½ to ¾ cup commercial sour cream
1 teaspoon dried dill weed
½ teaspoon salt
½ teaspoon ground black pepper
1½ pounds green cabbage, shredded
1 very large sweet red onion, thinly sliced crosswise and
    separated into rings

Stir together sour cream, dill, salt, and pepper; toss with cabbage and onion to mix well.

Variation: Substitute 1½ pounds Chinese cabbage (see preceding recipe), very thinly sliced crosswise, for green cabbage.

Sour Cream Slaw   6 to 7 servings

1 head green cabbage, shredded
2 large cucumbers, peeled and chopped
12 green onions with part of green tops, thinly sliced
½ cup sour cream or yogurt
2 tablespoons mayonnaise
1 tablespoon dried dill weed or crushed dill seeds
1 teaspoon salt
1 teaspoon ground black pepper

Put cabbage, cucumbers, and onions into a bowl. Stir together sour cream, mayonnaise, dill, salt, and pepper; toss with vegetables to mix well.

Cole Slaw   6 to 7 servings

Serve with spareribs or any other pork dish.

1 head green cabbage, finely shredded
1/3 cup white wine vinegar
2 tablespoons sugar
1 tablespoon snipped fresh tarragon leaves or about 1
    teaspoon crumbled dried tarragon
1 tablespoon *each* finely chopped green onions with part
    of green tops, dill weed, caraway seed, and prepared
    horseradish
½ teaspoon salt
About ¼ teaspoon black pepper
¼ teaspoon paprika
½ cup mayonnaise or yogurt

Toss cabbage with vinegar, and let stand for 1 hour. Drain, saving vinegar. Stir together drained vinegar and remaining ingredients to make a dressing. Add to cabbage, and toss thoroughly.

Hot Slaw **6 to 7 servings**

1 head green cabbage, cored and finely shredded
Boiling water
1 tablespoon butter
1 teaspoon salt
About ½ teaspoon black pepper
1 tablespoon wine vinegar
2 egg yolks
1 cup commercial sour cream
1 teaspoon sugar
½ teaspoon dry mustard

Cook cabbage in boiling water just until tender, about 5 minutes. Drain, and toss with butter, salt, and pepper. Sprinkle with vinegar, and keep warm. Beat together egg yolks, sour cream, sugar, and mustard. Add to cabbage, and cook and stir over low heat until sauce is slightly thickened; do not let it boil or it will separate.

Red and Green Cabbage **6 servings**

This tastes good for lunch on a hot day . . . beside a lake.

1 small head green cabbage, cored and finely shredded
1 small head red cabbage, cored and finely shredded
½ cup mayonnaise or yogurt
4 slices bacon, cooked until crisp and crumbled
½ pound liver sausage, diced

Toss green cabbage with half of the mayonnaise and half of the bacon. Toss red cabbage with remaining mayonnaise and bacon. Pile green cabbage with red cabbage alongside on serving plate or plates; surround with sausage dices.

Deviled Cabbage and Cucumber Salad   6 to 8 servings

3 hard-cooked eggs
1 tablespoon melted butter
1 tablespoon dry mustard
1 teaspoon salt
About ½ teaspoon black pepper
3 tablespoons wine or cider vinegar
½ cup light or heavy cream or yogurt
2 large cucumbers, peeled and diced
2 green onions with part of green tops, finely chopped
1 large head green cabbage, cored and finely shredded
Paprika

Separate egg yolks and whites. Slice whites. Mash egg yolks with butter, mustard, salt, and pepper; stir in vinegar and cream to make a dressing. Toss dressing thoroughly with egg whites, cucumbers, onions, and cabbage. Sprinkle with paprika.

Grapefruit and Onion Salad   6 servings

Serve with fish.

3 grapefruit
1 large sweet onion, very thinly sliced
1 teaspoon crumbled dried tarragon
About 3 tablespoons oil-and-vinegar dressing

Peel grapefruit and lift out sections, removing all white membrane. Sprinkle grapefruit and onions with tarragon, and toss with dressing.

Cabbage and Raisin Salad   6 servings

½ cup commercial sour cream
½ cup mayonnaise
½ teaspoon salt
½ teaspoon dill weed
1½ pounds red or green cabbage, cored and finely
    shredded
1¼ cups dark or golden raisins
1¼ cups chopped nuts (walnuts, peanuts, or pecans)

Stir together sour cream, mayonnaise, salt, and dill weed to make a dressing; toss thoroughly with remaining ingredients.

Variation: For the trail, prepare salad as directed above except substitute 6 ounces dehydrated cabbage for fresh. Soak cabbage in water to cover until tender. Substitute 1½ ounces packaged powdered sour cream sauce for commercial sour cream and mayonnaise. Prepare with water according to package directions, adding a little more water if necessary to thin to dressing consistency.

Carrot and Raisin Salad   6 servings

½ cup mayonnaise
1 tablespoon white wine vinegar or lemon juice
½ teaspoon salt
1½ pounds carrots, peeled, and coarsely shredded
1¼ cups raisins
1¼ cups chopped nuts (peanuts, walnuts, or pecans)

Stir together mayonnaise, vinegar, and salt to make a dressing. Toss thoroughly with remaining ingredients.

Variation: For the trail, follow recipe above *except* substitute 6 ounces dehydrated carrots for fresh. Soak carrots in water to cover until tender; drain.

Cucumber Salad 6 servings

¼ cup sour cream, or ¼ cup yogurt mixed with 1 table-
    spoon salad oil
2 tablespoons vinegar
1 teaspoon caraway seed
½ teaspoon *each* sugar, salt, and black pepper
6 medium-sized cucumbers, peeled and thinly sliced
    lengthwise
4 to 6 green onions with part of green tops, quartered
    lengthwise and cut into 2-inch lengths
2 green bell peppers, seeded and cut into thin lengthwise
    strips

Stir together sour cream, vinegar, caraway seeds, sugar,
salt, and pepper to make a dressing. Toss thoroughly
with remaining ingredients. Chill well.

Cucumbers, Radishes, and Onions 6 servings

¼ cup sour cream, or ¼ cup yogurt mixed with 1 table-
    spoon salad oil
1 tablespoon lemon juice
1 tablespoon sugar
About ¼ teaspoon salt
About ¼ teaspoon black pepper
6 cucumbers, peeled and thinly sliced crosswise
About 20 radishes, thinly sliced
2 or 3 green onions, with part of green tops, halved
    lengthwise and cut into 1-inch lengths

Stir together sour cream, lemon juice, sugar, salt and
pepper to make a dressing, and chill well; toss lightly
with remaining ingredients.

Eggplant Salad   6 servings

Serve on crisp lettuce leaves as a salad, or serve with sesame wafers as a dip.

1 large eggplant, peeled and cut into large chunks
Boiling salted water
1 large onion, finely chopped
2 large tomatoes, peeled, seeded, and diced
1/3 cup vinegar
2 tablespoons olive oil
1 tablespoon honey
About ½ teaspoon cayenne or curry powder

Cook eggplant in boiling salted water until tender. Drain, cool, and finely chop; mix with remaining ingredients. Turn into a stoneware or glass jar or bowl, cover, and chill for 24 hours.

Wilted Lettuce Salad   6 servings

3 or 4 heads green leafy lettuce such as garden lettuce,
    Australian, red leaf, butter (Boston), or romaine
    leaves
4 slices bacon, cut into small pieces
4 tablespoons cider or wine vinegar
½ teaspoon *each* salt, ground black pepper, and dry
    mustard

Break lettuce into bite-sized pieces into a bowl. Cook bacon until crisp; remove and drain on paper towels. Add remaining ingredients to bacon drippings, and cook, stirring to heat through and blend. Pour over lettuce, and toss to mix well. Top with bacon.

Variation: Substitute 1½ pounds green cabbage, finely shredded, for the lettuce.

Fruit Salad   6 servings

This salad is especially good with ham or pork dishes.
But it also goes well with any roasted meats. If you wish,
serve individual portions of it on lettuce leaves.

¼ cup salad oil
¼ cup fresh lemon juice
1 tablespoon finely chopped fresh parsley
1 tablespoon celery seed
1 teaspoon anise seed
½ teaspoon paprika
¼ teaspoon salt
2 apples, cut into thin wedge-slices
2 stalks celery, thinly sliced crosswise
4 bananas, sliced crosswise
1 fresh pineapple, peeled, cored, and cut into about
    1-inch chunks
1 papaya, peeled and cut into about 1-inch chunks
1 avocado, peeled and cut into about 1-inch chunks
1 cup chopped walnuts or pecans

Shake or beat together oil, lemon juice, parsley, celery
seed, anise seed, paprika, and salt to make a dressing;
toss with remaining ingredients.

Green Salad with Peas   6 servings

1 pound uncooked fresh garden peas or 1 pound frozen
    peas, thawed and drained
About 2 cups watercress sprigs
2 cups bean sprouts or alfalfa sprouts
2 tablespoons sesame oil
2 tablespoons lemon juice
About ¼ teaspoon salt

Gently toss all ingredients together.

Green Salad, Italian

This is good with boiled meats or broiled or roasted beef, lamb, or kid.

½ cup olive oil
1 sprig fresh mint, finely chopped
2 tablespoons capers
2 teaspoons finely snipped fresh basil or about 1 teaspoon crumbled dried basil
1 teaspoon salt
1 teaspoon anchovy paste or minced anchovies
About ¼ teaspoon black pepper
2 large green bell peppers, seeded and thinly sliced lengthwise
2 large sweet red bell peppers, seeded and thinly sliced lengthwise
6 stalks celery, sliced diagonally
6 green onions with part of green tops, halved lengthwise and cut into about 1-inch lengths
6 radishes, thinly sliced
4 large tomatoes, cut into wedges or sliced
About 1 cup small leafy sprigs of parsley (loosely pack to measure)
6 leaves romaine lettuce, broken

Shake or beat together oil, mint, capers, basil, salt, anchovies, and black pepper to make dressing. Toss with remaining ingredients.

Instant Potato Salad

6 or more servings

You can make this recipe with leftover boiled potatoes. Or make it from about 2 pounds of fresh potatoes. Serve it as a main dish for lunch or as an accompaniment salad for dinner.

3¼ ounces instant mashed potato powder
Boiling salted water
1 small onion or 6 green onions with part of green tops, minced (or 3 ounces dehydrated onion flakes, reconstituted)
1 long stalk celery, chopped (or 2 ounces dehydrated celery flakes, reconstituted)
2 dill pickles, chopped
4 tablespoons *each* mayonnaise, salad oil, and vinegar
3 tablespoons prepared mustard
2 teaspoons dried dill weed or seed
1 teaspoon *each* salt and ground black pepper

Prepare potatoes with boiling salted water according to package directions; do not use milk. Put potatoes, onions, celery, and pickles into a bowl. Stir together remaining ingredients, add to bowl, and toss to mix thoroughly. If necessary to moisten well, add a little more mayonnaise. Chill.

Alfalfa Sprouts for Salad   1 quart

Now! Grow your own greens while camping! Grow alfalfa sprouts!

Alfalfa sprouts can be eaten as is, or combined with other ingredients in salads. They are a concentrated source of nutrients, are easy to digest, and have good flavor. To get the fullest nutritional value, you should eat them within eight days of sprouting.

You will need a wide-mouthed quart jar with a lid; some sort of a screen (such as cheesecloth, fiberglass windowscreening, or piece of nylon stocking) to fit over the mouth of the jar as a strainer when rinsing the seeds; and a clear plastic bag of at least 1-quart capacity.

¼ cup alfalfa seeds
Water

Rinse seed in cool water until water runs clear. Put seeds into quart jar. Add enough warm (not hot) water to cover seeds by 2 inches. Fasten screen on top of jar. Allow seeds to stand for 4 hours. Drain off water. Rinse seeds again. Invert jar for a few minutes. Place in a warm, dark place — such as your knapsack. Rinse seeds twice a day for 3 or 4 days, until sprouts are 1 to 1½ inches long and have a "green" instead of a bean taste. Place in a clear plastic bag, and hang in filtered light for 1 or 2 days to allow chlorophyll to develop. Seal bag, and keep in a cool place such as a stream until eaten.

Variation: Substitute mungo beans or soy beans for the alfalfa seeds. (The bean sprouts called for in most oriental recipes derive from mungo beans.)

Molded Salmon Salad   6 servings

1 envelope unflavored gelatin
½ cup fresh lemon juice
2½ cups tomato juice
4 tablespoons prepared horseradish
1 tablespoon finely grated fresh onion
1 teaspoon salt
About 1/8 teaspoon black pepper
½ cup chopped celery
3 tablespoons chopped green bell pepper
1 can (1 pound) salmon, drained, skin and bones re-
    moved, and flaked
Mayonnaise

Sprinkle gelatin into lemon juice, and allow to soften.
Heat tomato juice to boiling, add to softened gelatin,
and stir until gelatin is completely dissolved. Stir in
horseradish, onion, salt, and black pepper. Fold in celery, green pepper, and salmon. Turn into mold or pan,
and chill until set. Unmold and/or cut into servings. Pass
mayonnaise.

Tomato Aspic   4 servings

Chill the can of aspic in a stream or ice chest before
serving.

1 can (13½ ounces) tomato aspic
About ½ cup mayonnaise
1 tablespoon drained capers

Slip aspic from can onto a pie tin. Combine mayonnaise
and capers, and spread evenly over curved surface of
aspic. Slice aspic, crosswise, into 4 pieces.

Variation: Substitute ½ teaspoon curry powder for the
capers.

Shrimp Salad

½ cup olive oil
¼ cup white wine vinegar
1 tablespoon dry mustard
1 teaspoon salt
1 pound raw shrimp, peeled and de-veined
2 medium-sized sweet onions, chopped
2 cucumbers, peeled and thinly sliced

Shake or beat together oil, vinegar, mustard, and salt to make a dressing. Combine shrimp, onions, cucumbers in a salad bowl; toss with just enough dressing to moisten well.

Variation: Substitute Shrimp Salad Dressing (page 156) for dressing above.

Tuna Salad

6 to 7 servings

To serve as a luncheon salad, prepare as written. To use as a sandwich filling, add a little more mayonnaise.

About 1½ pounds canned tuna packed in oil
6 stalks celery, finely chopped
4 dill pickles, minced
2 tablespoons crumbled dried tarragon
About 1 tablespoon salt
½ cup mayonnaise
¼ cup dry sherry or white table wine
2 tablespoons fresh lemon juice

Flake tuna with oil into a bowl. Add remaining ingredients. Toss to mix well.

Vegetable Salad

6 servings

1 head leafy lettuce
8 to 10 uncooked Brussels sprouts, very thinly sliced
2 medium-sized turnips, peeled and very thinly sliced
2 carrots, peeled and thinly sliced
Salt
Dill weed
½ cup salad oil
¼ cup white wine vinegar

Break lettuce leaves into salad bowl. Add Brussels sprouts, turnips, and carrots. Sprinkle with salt and dill weed to season. Toss with oil and vinegar.

Peas and Cheese Salad

6 servings

This is a good salad for lunch. You can make it of leftover peas and cheese.

2 cans (1 pound *each*) peas, drained, or 2 packages (10 ounces *each*) frozen peas, cooked just until tender
½ pound sharp Cheddar or longhorn cheese, diced
1 teaspoon crumbled dried basil
¼ teaspoon *each* salt and ground black pepper
½ cup mayonnaise

Chill peas. Put peas and cheese into a bowl. Sprinkle with basil, salt, and pepper. Add mayonnaise, and toss to mix well.

Flat Bread   About 6 servings

These thin, wafer-like rounds of bread keep well. You can eat them hot or cold as a meal accompaniment. Or for lunch, spread them with soft cheese or refried beans. If you wish a very firm, hard, cracker-like bread, knead the dough very thoroughly before shaping.

1 cup cool water
1 teaspoon cooking oil
1 teaspoon salt
About 3 cups whole wheat flour
½ cup powdered milk (optional)

Mix together all ingredients in a bowl to make a stiff dough. Pinch off a large or small piece of dough, pat out to a 1/8-inch-thick flat tortilla-like round. Lightly dust the round with flour. Lightly oil a heavy frying pan; brown the round on both sides in pan over a low fire. Repeat to use all dough.

Ham Biscuits or Ham Corn Bread   6 or more servings

To assemble each serving: Break open a biscuit or two or a square of corn bread, top with 2 poached eggs, and cover with Cheese Sauce (see under Medium Cream Sauce, page 152).

½ cup finely diced cooked smoked ham
1 recipe Buttermilk Biscuits (page 144) or Golden Corn
    Bread (page 145)

Stir ham into dry ingredients for either biscuits or corn bread, then finish biscuits or corn bread as directed.

Buttermilk Biscuits   About 16 biscuits

2 cups flour
4 teaspoons baking powder
½ teaspoon salt
¼ teaspoon baking soda
¾ cup buttermilk
¼ cup cooking oil or melted shortening

Sift together into a mixing bowl the flour, baking powder, salt, and soda. Mix buttermilk and oil, add to bowl, and toss with a fork to mix. Turn out onto a floured board. Shape into a log, and pinch off portions of dough to form biscuits about 2 to 3 inches in diameter and ½ inch thick. Or pat or roll dough to ½ inch thickness, and cut into biscuits with a 2- to 3-inch circle cutter. At camp: Brush biscuit tops and bottoms with oil. Arrange over bottom of a greased Dutch oven, cover, bury in hot coals, and bake for about 15 minutes. At home: Place on a greased baking sheet, and bake in a very hot oven (475°) for about 12 minutes or until golden brown.

Variation: Use packaged refrigerated buttermilk biscuits, and bake in Dutch oven as directed above or, at home, according to package directions. These packaged biscuits must be kept well insulated in picnic box or backpack.

Golden Corn Bread

6 or more servings

1½ cups yellow corn meal
½ cup flour
1 tablespoon sugar
4 teaspoons baking powder
½ teaspoon salt
1 egg, beaten
1 cup milk
¼ cup melted shortening or cooking oil
Butter

Sift corn meal, flour, sugar, baking powder, and salt together into a bowl. Beat together egg, milk, and shortening. Add to bowl, and beat just until mixture is smooth — no more than 1 minute. Pour into a greased frying pan (about 10-inch) or 9-inch-square baking pan. At camp: Cover or wrap with double thickness of heavy foil. Bury in hot coals, and bake for about 30 minutes. At home: Bake in a hot oven (425°) for 20 to 25 minutes or until golden brown. Cut while hot, split pieces open, and spread with butter.

Poppyseed Drop Biscuits 14 to 16 biscuits

1½ cups flour
½ cup corn meal
3 teaspoons baking powder
1 teaspoon salt
2 tablespoons shredded or grated Parmesan cheese
1 tablespoon poppy seeds
¼ cup cooking oil
1 cup milk

Sift flour, corn meal, baking powder, and salt together into a mixing bowl. Stir in cheese, poppy seeds, and oil. Gradually add milk, and stir lightly to mix. At camp: Drop by tablespoonfuls onto greased shallow pan and bake in reflector oven until golden brown. Or drop over bottom of greased Dutch oven, brush tops with oil, cover oven, bury in hot coals, and bake for about 20 minutes. At home: Drop onto a greased baking sheet, and bake in a very hot oven (450°) for 12 to 15 minutes or until golden brown.

Corn Pone Bread

This is the old-time hoe cake, meant to be cooked in the coals of the fireplace or campfire. It is not a critical formula, so you can bake pones satisfactorily in various kinds of coals at various heats.

2 cups yellow corn meal
1 teaspoon salt
½ cup small pieces pork crackling or crisply cooked
    bacon, crumbled
Boiling water
1 tablespoon cooking oil or bacon drippings

Stir together corn meal, salt, and cracklings. Gradually stir in enough boiling water to make the mixture a thick paste. Add oil, and mix in well with hands. Shape between palms into ovals about 2 by 3 inches and ½-inch thick. Arrange over bottom of greased Dutch oven, cover, bury in hot coals and bake for about 45 minutes. Or place on greased griddle set onto coals and bake until cooked through.

Be sure that the liquid beneath the cooking dumplings only simmers. Do not allow it to boil because that vigorous agitation could break the dumplings into pieces.

2 cups flour
4 teaspoons baking powder
1 teaspoon salt
1½ teaspoons cooking oil
About ¾ cup milk
Simmering broth, soup, or stew

Sift flour, baking powder, and salt together into a bowl. Stir in oil and enough milk to make a stiff dough. Pat or roll out dough to ½- to 1-inch thickness. With a sharp knife, cut into 1- to 2-inch squares. Drop dumplings onto simmering broth. Cover, and simmer for 20 minutes.

Variation: Instead of mixing dumpling dough, use packaged refrigerator biscuits. Cut each biscuit in half, drop onto simmering liquid, cover, and simmer for 20 minutes.

Sourdough Starter for Pancakes

Sourdough starter is ready to use when it bubbles. The time it takes to reach the bubbling stage will vary according to the temperature.

1 cake compressed yeast
2 cups water at room temperature
1 tablespoon sugar
1 teaspoon salt
2 cups flour
Pancake addition (recipe below)

Crumble yeast into water in a 4-quart crock. Stir in sugar, salt, and flour. Cover, and let stand at room temperature or slightly warmer until mixture bubbles, about 3 to 4 days. The night before making pancakes, stir in pancake addition and enough more water (if necessary) to make a thick paste. Cover, and let mixture stand at room temperature overnight. Mixture will become thinner. In the morning, pour off 4 cups of the mixture to use for making pancakes (see recipe page 150). Put remaining mixture into a jar or crock, cover, and keep refrigerated or very well chilled. This mixture is the continuing starter. In order to keep it alive and for best results, use it and replenish it with pancake addition every week. To hold for a longer time, freeze. Before use, allow to thaw, and let stand at room temperature for 24 hours after thawing.

Pancake addition. Stir together 2 cups flour, 1 tablespoon sugar, ½ teaspoon salt, and 2 cups water..

Note: If you should be in camp without yeast, you can make sourdough starter by substituting an additional 4 tablespoons sugar and 1½ teaspoons salt for the yeast. The mixture will then require about 5 days to bubble and be ready for use.

Sourdough Pancakes

About 18 pancakes
or 6 servings

4 cups dough from sourdough crock
1 egg, beaten (optional)
3 tablespoons melted bacon drippings or cooking oil
2 tablespoons sugar
1 teaspoon salt
Water if necessary
1 teaspoon baking soda dissolved in 1 tablespoon water

Stir together dough, egg, oil, sugar, and salt. If necessary to thin batter to proper pouring consistency for medium-thin pancakes, add a little water. Mix well. Stir in soda and water; do not beat mixture further. Pour batter into 3- to 4-inch circles on a hot, lightly greased griddle. Bake pancakes until golden brown on both sides.

Sourdough Pancakes with Blueberries   6 servings

Top with syrup (or honey) heated with butter — about 1 cup liquid to 3 tablespoons butter.

About 12 ounces sourdough pancake mix, prepared
    according to package directions
1½ cups fresh blueberries or 1½ cups canned, drained
    blueberries

Stir blueberries into pancake batter. Spoon onto greased and heated griddle, and bake as for other pancakes.

Apple Pancakes

Top pancakes with melted butter and honey. Accompany with crisp bacon or browned sausages.

2 medium-sized apples, peeled, cored, and sliced cross-
    wise about 1/8 inch thick
Butter
About 2 12-ounce packages pancake mix, prepared ac-
    cording to package directions

Place several apple slices well apart on buttered, heated griddle. Lightly brown on bottom side, then turn. Pour enough pancake batter over each slice to cover. When pancakes are brown on the bottom, turn and brown on second side. Repeat to use all apples and batter.

Sauces, Condiments, Dressings

Thin Cream Sauce

One of the best camp uses of this sauce is for making a cream soup from a soup mix: Substitute cream sauce for each cup of water called for in preparing the mix.

1 tablespoon butter
1 tablespoon flour
1 cup milk
¼ teaspoon salt
About 1/8 teaspoon black pepper

Melt butter, and stir in flour to make a smooth paste. Gradually add milk, cooking and stirring to make a smooth and thickened sauce. Season with salt and pepper.

Medium Cream Sauce

To change this from a cream sauce to a cream gravy, substitute meat drippings for the butter. To change it from a cream sauce to a cream-style curry sauce, add curry powder to taste. To make it into a cheese sauce, add 3 to 4 ounces shredded sharp Cheddar cheese and a dash of Tabasco.

2 tablespoons butter
2 tablespoons flour
1 cup milk
¼ teaspoon salt
About 1/8 teaspoon black pepper

Melt butter, and stir in flour to make a smooth paste. Gradually add milk, cooking and stirring to make a smooth and thickened sauce. Season with salt and pepper.

Mushroom Sauce

For vegetables or meats.

½ cup sliced onions
2 tablespoons butter
1 clove garlic, minced or mashed
½ pound fresh mushrooms, thinly sliced
1 tablespoon cornstarch
½ cup water
½ teaspoon lemon juice
Salt

Sauté onions in butter until limp. Stir in garlic and mushrooms. Stir together cornstarch, water, and lemon juice, and add to onions-mushrooms. Cook, stirring, until mushrooms are tender and liquid is glossy, about 5 minutes. Add salt to taste.

Salsa Caliente (Hot Sauce)   About 2½ cups

Serve with Mexican beans, enchiladas, or tamales.

1 can (about 1 pound) tomato purée or tomato sauce
2 tablespoons vinegar
2 tablespoons salad oil
3 tablespoons minced onions
2·canned green chilis, chopped
3 dried chili *tepines*, crushed, or about ¾ teaspoon
    crushed dried hot red peppers
1 tablespoon crumbled dried oregano
1 teaspoon salt
Cayenne or Tabasco

Stir together all ingredients, seasoning with cayenne or Tabasco according to degree of hotness you wish.

Camper's Roux

A roux is used to thicken broth, soup, or stews.

Work together well to make a blended mixture, equal parts of soft butter and flour. Wrap in waxed paper or plastic to carry to camp. Cut off a portion of the roux as needed.

Drop roux into bubbling liquid, and stir until liquid is thickened. A portion of roux containing 1 tablespoon of flour will slightly thicken 1 cup of liquid; a portion of roux containing 2 tablespoons flour will thicken 1 cup liquid to medium-thick consistency.

Camper's Chutney*   6 servings

You can combine all the ingredients except water for this chutney at home, carry it to camp, and cook it there to serve with a curry. You serve this chutney along with other condiments to be added to curried meat and rice as the eater wishes.

8 ounces freeze-dried fruit mix or dried apples
2 ounces instant minced dried onions or onion flakes
¼ cup brown sugar or honey
2 tablespoons dry mustard
1 tablespoon ground coriander
About 1½ teaspoons ground ginger
1 teaspoon *each* salt, garlic powder, and turmeric
½ teaspoon *each* cayenne and ground cloves

In a kettle, combine all ingredients with enough water to just cover. Allow to stand until fruits are reconstituted. Heat to boiling, then simmer, covered, stirring occasionally for about 30 minutes or until fruit is tender and mixture has blended to a thick, sweet-hot sauce. Cool.

*A recipe for Chutney for 20 appears in *Food for Knapsackers*.

154

Vegetable Sauce

Serve with cooked broccoli or Brussels sprouts, or over a wedge of steamed cabbage.

1 tablespoon cornstarch
1 tablespoon water
1 cup yogurt
1 teaspoon mashed capers
½ teaspoon *each* salt and turmeric

In a heavy saucepan, stir cornstarch and water together until smooth. Add remaining ingredients, and mix well. Cook over low heat, stirring, until thickened and smooth.

Fruit Compote for Pancakes

Topping or filling
for 6 servings

8 ounces freeze-dried fruit mix (Fruit Galaxy) or vacuum-dried fruit mix or 10 ounces mixed dried fruits
2 cups water
1¼ cups brown sugar, firmly packed, or honey
1 teaspoon ground nutmeg
1 teaspoon ground cloves
½ teaspoon grated fresh lemon peel

Combine all ingredients in a saucepan, and simmer, covered, stirring occasionally, until fruit is tender and mixture is blended to a thick syrup-sauce, about 15 minutes. Serve warm or when cooled.

Fresh Peach Sauce   **Topping or filling for
                                           about 6 servings**

Serve this sauce warm, as a topping for pancakes or as a
filling for rolled or folded Sourdough Pancakes (page 150)
or omelets.

1½ cups sugar
½ cup water
Dash of salt
2 cups sliced fresh peaches

In a saucepan, heat sugar, water, and salt to boiling. Add
peaches, and simmer until they are just tender, about 10
to 15 minutes.

Shrimp Salad Dressing   **About 1 cup**

This recipe is intended for shrimp salad, but it dresses
other seafood salads well, too.

¾ cup mayonnaise
2 tablespoons liquid drained from pickled peppers or
    vinegar
1 tablespoon prepared horseradish
1 tablespoon dry mustard
1 teaspoon crumbled dried thyme
¼ teaspoon salt
Dash of Tabasco

Mix all ingredients together well.

Caper Mayonnaise for Poached Salmon   About 1¼ cups

1 cup mayonnaise
1 tablespoon dry mustard
2 tablespoons drained capers
1 tablespoon *each* snipped chives, crumbled dried
    thyme, crumbled dried chervil, and fresh lemon juice

Stir together mayonnaise and mustard until smooth. Stir
in remaining ingredients.

Cooked Salad Dressing

You can vary this dressing by adding sour cream, horseradish, or finely chopped hard-cooked eggs.

4 tablespoons sugar
4 tablespoons flour
2 teaspoons salt
2 teaspoons dry mustard
Dash of cayenne
4 egg yolks, beaten
1½ cups milk
½ cup white vinegar
2 tablespoons butter

In top of double boiler (or small saucepan set into another pan), stir together sugar, flour, salt, mustard, and
cayenne. Stir in egg yolks and milk. Place over hot
water, and cook, stirring, until mixture is thick and
smooth. Stir in vinegar and butter, and allow to cool;
stirring occasionally.

Desserts

Specific recipes follow, but consider also these general dessert ideas:

Seasonal fresh fruits with cheeses. Good fruit cheeses for camping include Cheddar, Monterey Jack, Tybo, Kumin-Ost, blue, and Gouda. Good cheese fruits are apples, grapes, pears, apricots, peaches, and nectarines.

Packaged mixes for cake, sweet breads, and pies purchased in a supermarket and prepared in camp.

Stewed dried fruits seasoned with sweet spices, honey, or brown sugar and served either hot or cold.

Packaged dried mincemeat eaten directly from the package — for a nourishing dessert when ski-touring or snowshoeing.

Sautéed Bananas   6 servings

6 ripe-but-firm bananas, peeled and halved lengthwise
About 2 tablespoons honey
About 2 tablespoons butter
1 cup applesauce
Ground nutmeg

Roll banana pieces in honey to coat. Sauté in butter over medium-high heat until golden on both sides. Remove to serving plates. Serve with a topping of applesauce sprinkled with nutmeg.

Camp Baked Apples

6 servings

6 unpeeled tart cooking apples, cored
Water
6 tablespoons ginger marmalade, orange marmalade,
  honey mixed with cinnamon, small cinnamon candies, or tart sugared berries for filling
Heavy cream, whipped cream, or ice cream

Place apples in a Dutch oven. Add enough water to just
cover bottom of oven. Put 1 tablespoon filling in core
cavity of each apple. Cover oven, bury in coals, and
allow apples to cook for about 30 minutes or until tender. Serve with cream or ice cream.

Dessert Fruit Salad

6 servings

¼ cup fresh lemon juice
2 tablespoons sherry
2 tablespoons honey
1 teaspoon celery seed
¼ teaspoon salt
2 papayas, peeled and cut into about 1-inch chunks
1 small fresh pineapple, peeled, cored, and cut into
  about 1-inch chunks
4 bananas, peeled, cut into ½-inch crosswise slices
1 large apple, cut into thin wedge-slices
1 cup coarsely chopped walnuts

Beat together lemon juice, sherry, honey, celery seed,
and salt to make a dressing; toss gently with remaining
ingredients.

Chocolate Frosting   **Topping for 8-inch loaf cake**

Use to top a chocolate or mocha loaf cake — home-baked, made from mix, or purchased.

1 square (1 ounce) unsweetened baking chocolate,
    melted over hot water
1 egg, beaten
1 tablespoon heavy cream
1 teaspoon vanilla
About 1¾ cups unsifted powdered sugar
¼ cup chopped walnuts

Beat warm chocolate into egg. Stir in cream and vanilla. Gradually add powdered sugar, beating to make a smooth mixture. Spread onto cake. Sprinkle with nuts.

Pie Pastry   **One 9-inch pie shell**

1 cup flour
3/8 teaspoon salt
½ cup lard or hydrogenated vegetable shortening
¼ cup cold water

Stir or sift flour and salt together into a mixing bowl. With pastry blender, two knives, or clean fingers, cut or rub shortening until particles are the size of small peas. Add cold water and toss with a fork to mix. Gather together to make a ball. On a lightly floured board, roll out to a thin circle to fit a 9-inch pie pan.

Variation: Use prepared pastry mix and prepare according to package instructions.

Pound Cake and Fruit   6 servings

Pound cake is a good camp cake simply to serve alone. It
also goes very well with fruits, shortcake-style.

12 thin slices pound cake
About 1 quart fresh strawberries or raspberries
Sugar or honey
1 cup heavy whipping cream or substitute whipped
    cream topping
1 tablespoon light or dark rum

Rinse and drain berries. Hull strawberries and slice.
Sweeten berries with a little sugar or honey to taste.
Whip cream, adding rum. For each serving: Put 1 slice
cake on a plate, top with a spoonful of berries, top with
another cake slice, more berries, and whipped cream.

Variations: 1) Substitute canned fruits such as cherries,
peaches, apricots, or plums for berries.
   2) Substitute freeze-dried fruit (1 ounce per person)
for berries. Reconstitute freeze-dried fruit in white wine
or in a mixture of half water-half wine.

Coffee Pudding   8 or more servings

2 cans (15 ounces *each*) sweetened condensed milk
2 packages (3¼ ounces *each*) vanilla pudding and pie
    filling mix
4 tablespoons instant coffee powder
4 tablespoons brandy or 6 tablespoons sherry
Whipped cream

Combine milk, pudding powder and coffee in a saucepan, and cook and stir over medium heat until mixture is
thickened and smooth. Stir in brandy or sherry. Chill.
Serve topped with whipped cream.

Pineapple Upside-Down Cake   9 servings

1 can (1 pound 4 ounces) pineapple slices; or 1 small
    fresh pineapple, peeled, cored, and cut into ¼-inch-
    thick crosswise slices with 1 to 2 tablespoons brown
    sugar or honey
1 package (about 1 pound) white cake mix, prepared
    according to package directions
Whipped cream

Arrange canned pineapple slices in a single layer over
bottom of a 9-inch square cake pan, and spoon 2 to 3
tablespoons of the syrup over them; or arrange fresh
pineapple slices the same way and top with sugar or
honey. Pour prepared cake batter evenly over pineapple.
At home: Bake according to cake-package directions. At
camp: Cover pan with double thickness of heavy foil;
bury in coals; and bake for about 40 minutes or until
cake springs back when touched with fingertip. While
warm or when cooled, cut cake into squares and serve
pineapple side up, topped with whipped cream.

Sand Tarts   About 40 cookies

1 cup soft butter
1 teaspoon vanilla
3 tablespoons powdered sugar
1 cup ground almonds
2½ cups sifted cake flour

Stir all ingredients together with a wooden spoon to
make a firm dough. Pinch off walnut size pieces of
dough and form into about ¼-inch-thick crescents. In
camp: Place on griddle set over very low heat, and bake
until cooked through. At home: Place on ungreased baking sheet, and bake in a slow oven (325°) for 15 to 18
minutes or until golden. Cool on rack.

Peach Cobbler

6 servings

1 egg
½ cup sugar
½ teaspoon grated fresh lemon peel
1 teaspoon vanilla
1 cup flour
1 teaspoon baking powder
½ teaspoon salt
¼ cup milk
¼ cup melted butter
1 large can (1 pound 13 ounces) sliced peaches, drained;
    or 3 cups thawed frozen peaches
About ½ cup brown sugar firmly packed
About 2 tablespoons lemon juice
Sour cream sprinkled with nutmeg

Beat together egg, sugar, lemon peel and vanilla. Stir or sift together flour, baking powder and salt; add to egg mixture alternately with the milk, beating after each addition. Stir in butter.

In camp: Spread over bottom of a buttered Dutch oven or 9-inch square baking pan. Arrange peaches over top. Sprinkle with brown sugar and lemon juice. Cover with its lid; cover baking pan with double thickness of heavy foil. Bury in coals and bake for about 1 hour. At home: Assemble in a buttered 9-inch square pan; bake in a moderate oven (350°) for 1 hour or until cake pulls away from sides of pan. Spoon out while still warm and top with sour cream.

Variation: Substitute 2 cups fresh or frozen blueberries for peaches. Sprinkle with granulated sugar to sweeten and about ½ teaspoon ground cinnamon instead of brown sugar and lemon juice.

Shortbread   **About 50 cookies**

Bake shortbread at home and take it to camp.

1 pound (2 cups) soft butter
1 cup unsifted powdered sugar
1 teaspoon vanilla
5 cups sifted all-purpose flour

In a mixing bowl, cream together butter and sugar. Beat in vanilla. Stir in flour. Pat on a lightly floured board to about ¼-inch thickness. Cut into circles with a 2-inch biscuit cutter. Place on a baking sheet. Bake in a slow oven (325°) for 18 minutes or until golden. Cool on a rack.

Molasses Chocolate Cooky Squares   **32 squares**

¼ cup molasses
½ cup butter or margarine
¾ cup brown sugar firmly packed
½ teaspoon baking soda
1 egg, beaten
1 cup flour
½ teaspoon salt
4 ounces semi-sweet chocolate, finely chopped

Heat molasses and butter together in a saucepan until butter melts. Add brown sugar and soda, and cook and stir until sugar dissolves. Remove from heat and allow to cool. Then add egg, flour, salt and chocolate; stir to mix well. Spread batter evenly over bottom of 2 buttered 8-inch-square baking pans. At camp: Cover each pan with a double thickness of foil, bury in coals and bake for about 45 minutes. At home: Bake in a moderate oven (350°) for 20 to 25 minutes. Cut into 2-inch squares. Cool in pan on a rack.

Apple Pie   6 to 8 servings

Pastry for double-crust 9-inch pie
6 tart cooking apples, cored and thinly sliced
1 cup brown sugar, firmly packed
1 tablespoon ground cinnamon
1 tablespoon ground nutmeg
1 teaspoon fresh lemon juice
1 teaspoon butter
Sharp Cheddar cheese or vanilla ice cream

Line a 9-inch pie pan with one pastry circle. Fill with apples. Sprinkle apples with brown sugar, cinnamon, nutmeg and lemon juice; dot with butter. Cover with top crust, cut with a decorative vent; flute pastry edges together to seal well.

At camp: Place pie in a Dutch oven and cover, or wrap pie in a double thickness of heavy foil. Bury in coals, and bake for about 1 hour. At home: Bake in a very hot oven (450°) for 10 minutes, then reduce heat to 425° and bake for about 30 minutes more or until crust is well browned. Cool partially on a rack. Serve while hot with cheese or ice cream.

Coffee Cream Sauce   Topping for about 6 servings

Serve as a topping for pieces of loaf cake, especially chocolate and mocha ones.

¼ cup sugar
¼ cup strong black coffee
1 cup heavy cream, whipped

In a heavy pan, stir sugar over low heat until it melts into a syrup. Remove from heat and slowly add coffee. Return to heat and boil and stir until blended. Cool. Fold in whipped cream.

165

English Fruit Cake 2 loaf cakes

Bake at home and take to camp.

½ cup soft butter or margarine
1 cup granulated sugar
1 cup brown sugar, firmly packed
5 eggs
1 teaspoon almond extract
3 cups sifted all-purpose flour
½ teaspoon *each* salt, baking soda, ground mace, and
    ground cinnamon
½ cup grape juice
3 cups golden raisins
2 cups dark seedless raisins
1 cup dried currants
1 cup coarsely chopped blanched almonds
1 cup coarsely chopped walnuts or pecans
1 cup glacéed cherries, halved
¾ cup chopped candied citron
½ cup chopped candied lemon peel
8 slices candied pineapple, cut into small wedges
Port or red table wine

In a large mixing bowl, cream together thoroughly butter, granulated sugar, and brown sugar. Add eggs, one at a time, beating well after each addition. Beat in almond extract. Sift together flour, salt, soda, mace, and cinnamon. Add to mixing bowl alternately with grape juice, beating after each addition and beginning and ending with dry ingredients. Thoroughly mix in remaining ingredients except wine.

Press into 2 well-greased 9- by 5-inch bread loaf pans. Bake in a very slow oven (275°) for 2 hours. Cool in pans on a rack for 30 minutes. Remove from pans, and let cool thoroughly on rack. Wrap each loaf in a cloth which has been moistened with wine. Store in an airtight container at room or cellar temperature for several weeks; remoisten cloths with wine occasionally. Slice thinly to serve.

Apricot Pie   6 servings

Pastry for double-crust 8-inch pie
2 cups drained canned apricot halves
1 cup brown sugar, firmly packed, or 1 cup honey
1 tablespoon ground cinnamon
1 tablespoon ground allspice
1 teaspoon fresh lemon juice
1 teaspoon butter

Line an 8-inch pie pan with one pastry circle. Fill with apricots. Sprinkle with sugar, cinnamon, allspice, and lemon juice; dot with butter. Cover with top crust, cut with decorative vent; flute pastry edges together to seal well.

At camp: Place pie in a Dutch oven and cover, or wrap pie in a double thickness of heavy foil. Bury in coals, and bake for about 1 hour. At home: Bake in a very hot oven (450°) for 10 minutes, then reduce heat to 425° and bake for about 30 minutes more or until crust is well browned. Cool on a rack.

Variations: 1) Dried apricot pie: Follow directions above except substitute 2 cups drained and barely cooked dried apricots for canned, and sprinkle apricots additionally with about 3 tablespoons apricot cooking juices.

2) Fresh apricot pie: Follow directions above except substitute 2½ cups halved and pitted fresh apricots for canned, and sprinkle apricots with an additional 1/3 cups sugar, 2 teaspoons lemon juice and 3 tablespoons water (as well as ingredients listed above).

Wild Rose Hip Soup   6 to 8 servings

The packaged powder for rose hip soup is available in gourmet shops, health food stores, and specialty food sections of some supermarkets.

2 packages (4½ ounces *each*) wild rose hip soup powder
2 cups water
6 to 8 rusks or Zwieback
Whipped cream

Prepare soup according to package directions *except* use only 2 cups water. To serve: Place a rusk in each bowl, pour soup over, and top with whipped cream.

Camp Coffee   Makes about 12 coffee cups

Camp coffee should be strong. Have boiling water available for people who want a weaker brew; don't dilute the central pot.

8 ounces (about 2½ cups) regular-grind coffee
Cold water
Pinch of salt

Combine coffee, 7 cups water, and salt in a pot or kettle. Bring to boiling, then gently boil for 5 minutes. Remove from heat. Add ½ cup cold water (to settle the grounds). Serve immediately. Or keep hot at side of the fire.

Variation: Use above proportions and this method: Add coffee and salt to boiling water, cover, and boil for 3 minutes. Remove from heat, and add cold water.

Note about coffee in large quantities:
To make the best coffee, plan on no more than 35 coffee-cup servings from 1 pound of coffee (use 6½ quarts water). To make good but not great coffee, make 40 coffee-cup servings from 1 pound of coffee (use 7½ quarts water). Extending 1 pound of coffee any further will result in a weak, flavorless mixture. Choose a pot or kettle large enough to allow coffee plenty of space to swell during brewing. Cut a double-gauze diaper in half to make 2 coffee sacks; tie measured coffee in diaper-half with twine. Follow either of the above two methods.

Tea

Calculate quantity tea-making by these proportions:

Tea bags: 1 tea bag and 1 measuring cup of water for
  each person plus 1 extra cup of water for the pot.
Loose tea: 1 teaspoon tea and 1 measuring cup of water
  for each person plus 1 extra cup of water for the pot.

Use any good black tea such as English Breakfast or Irish
tea or orange pekoe, or green tea, or spiced tea.

To make tea: Heat water just to boiling. Pour over tea,
and allow to steep for 1 to 5 minutes, depending on how
strong you wish the tea. (Remove tea bags.)

Variations: 1) Add 1 or 2 teaspoons brandy to a cup of
hot tea. Especially good on a cold day or after skiing or
snowshoeing.
  2) Make iced tea of leftover hot tea brewed earlier in
the day.

Mexican Chocolate   **1 serving**

Make no more than two or three cups of chocolate at a
time.

1 1-inch square Mexican chocolate (or use 1 tablespoon
  cocoa powder and about 1/8 teaspoon ground
  cinnamon)
1 cup milk

Put chocolate and milk into a deep saucepan, and slowly
heat to boiling; then simmer for 10 minutes. Remove
from heat. Beat mixture by whirling a Mexican wooden
beater (*molinillo*) or a wire whisk between palms of
hands until mixture is foamy. Serve immediately.

Mocha
1 serving

1 tablespoon instant coffee powder or freeze-dried
coffee
1 teaspoon milk cocoa powder (with milk and sugar in
it)
1 cup boiling water

Put coffee and cocoa into a large mug. Add water, and
stir to dissolve cocoa and coffee.

Cappuccino
1 serving

Some say that because Demerara is high-proof rum (150
to 160 proof), it is the most practical rum to take
backpacking or camping. But you can use any dark rum
such as Jamaica in this recipe.

1 teaspoon milk cocoa powder (with milk and sugar in
it)
1 teaspoon freeze-dried coffee or instant coffee powder
1 cup boiling water
1 tablespoon dark rum or brandy

Put cocoa and coffee into a large mug. Add water, and
stir until cocoa and coffee are dissolved. Add rum or
brandy.

Carob Drink
1 serving

This is a nutritious substitute for hot chocolate.

2 to 6 tablespoons carob powder
4 to 6 tablespoons milk powder
1 cup boiling water
Honey

In a mug, mix carob powder and milk powder well.
Gradually stir in water. Add honey to taste.

Peppermint Tea   1 serving

This is especially soothing for an upset stomach.

1 cup boiling water
1 tablespoon crumbled dried peppermint leaves

Let water cool just until it is not boiling. Pour over
peppermint, and let stand for 5 minutes. Strain into a
mug or cup.

Other Hot Beverages for Camp

Prepare according to package directions.

Yerba Maté (South American herb tea)
Sassafras bark tea
Herb tea

Other Cold Beverages for Camp

Purchase in camping or mountaineering stores or in
grocery stores.
Prepare according to package directions.

Apple cider
Grapefruit juice (from freeze-dried crystals)
Orange juice (from freeze-dried crystals)
Tomato juice (from freeze-dried crystals)
Iced coffee (from freeze-dried powder)
Iced tea (from freeze-dried powder)

Other Stronger Beverages for Camp

Mountain Lemonade: In a cup, stir a little lemonade concentrate powder with snow or icy stream water; add 1 teaspoon 190-proof alcohol.

Restorative after a hard day of travel and before the soup is ready: Put a dollop of 151-proof Demerara rum (light or dark) in a cup of any fruit juice, tea, or coffee.

Mountain Mint Julep: Crush a few leaves of pennyroyal or other wild mint in a cup, add a dollop of spirits of any strength (90- to 190-proof), and top with ½ cup snow, or icy stream water.

Appendix

Much of the material in the Appendix has been distilled from *Food for Knapsackers*, published in 1971 by the Sierra Club. The information is pertinent. We include it here for the benefit of campers who do not have immediate access to that book.

Packaging the Food

These instructions might also be called "repackaging" instructions, because you should repackage just about everything edible for your trip. You will need a large supply of plastic bags — pint-sized ones to hold small quantities, quart-sized ones for larger quantities — some plastic bottles, rubber bands or plastic-wire ties, and a felt marking pen.

When tying plastic bags, push all the air out before you fasten them. That way the bags are less likely to break open.

In general, the contents of each bag should serve for only one meal. That is, if you're planning to serve chocolate pudding twice, make up 2 bags of chocolate pudding.

Repackage all cereals, beverages, puddings, and powders in double plastic bags. Include a label with instructions for preparation, and a notation of the total amount of whatever is inside each one. On the outside of the bag write with your marking pen the date and meal for which the contents are intended. *Label everything.*

Wherever possible for any particular recipe, try to combine the dry ingredients — meat, vegetables, seasonings — and put them together in a single bag. That way you will be ahead of the game in camp, needing only to complete the recipe directions.

Packaged soups need not be emptied from their envelopes before insertion in bags.

Beverages and staples can be sacked together in bulk quantities for convenience, rather than divided into individual meals. Or if your trip will be more than 1 week long, these items can be divided into 1-week periods, and marked accordingly. You also can put coffee, instant tea, powdered milk, sugar and other staples, into plastic nursing bottles, 4- or 8-ounce size. Glue the lid inside the rim; label the bottle. (You can carry liquids in nursing bottles if you are careful to use the nipple or some other gasket under the lid.)

Canned foods and boxes of crackers should be tied into plastic bags and marked with the day and meal when they will be served.

All cheese should be left in its wax coating. If the kind you're taking has been cut, the best seal will be a thickness of cheesecloth, followed by a quick dip into hot paraffin. Protected this way and stored in a cool place, cheese will keep indefinitely. If the cheese is to be eaten early in your trip, you can wrap it in waxed paper or cheesecloth. Then into plastic bags. Salami and cheese may both mold a bit; merely scrape off the mold before eating.

Butter is best carried packed in a tin. Try to keep it in a cool place. But you can package margarine boxes in separate plastic bags.

Oil, vinegar, and other dressings should all be put into plastic bottles with tight screw lids. Then into separate plastic bags.

Tips for Backpackers

Backpacking becomes increasingly simple with the variety of lightweight food proliferating in the markets. Yet there is no real reason to neglect fresh food entirely. It always tastes delicious on the trail. Some fresh fruits and vegetables are good travelers — apples, celery, cabbage, carrots, oranges. And they add only a little bulk and weight to your backpack.

If your trip is to be a weekend one, you can make stew at home, freeze it in plastic bags or cartons, keep it in a picnic box or freezer-bag on the way to the hike, and then transfer it (well wrapped) into your pack. The meat will thaw slowly during the day until it is just right for cooking when you reach camp.

Canned food is practical for weekend hikes, but be careful to purchase only solid-pack meat, a minimum of any liquid, and no cream sauces. Otherwise you will be carrying unnecessary weight.

Many packaged sauces can be found on grocery shelves: sour cream sauce, à la king, spaghetti, chili, and a variety of salad dressings.

Health food stores can provide a variety of goodies such as freshly ground peanut butter (and other nut butters) that will add interest to a hiker's lunch. These stores are also a source of various teas: peppermint, sassafras, fenugreek, alfalfa. Buy some of each; on the trip prepare a different tea each day.

Water: Everybody's liquid intake varies. But as a minimum, for desert or dry country backpacking, each person will need a 1-gallon canteen or 2 ½-gallon canteens (or plastic jugs). One and one-half gallons are better . . . Wherever you go, take along a water purifier. Nowadays all rivers, lakes, and streams, even in the high mountains, have some coliform count. . . . Always soak and cook foods in the same water.

You can make a satisfactory instant breakfast from packaged milkshake, dried apricots, jerky and pilot crackers.

And remember: careful packaging (and repackaging) is the formula for a successful trip. At home, package the exact amounts of food for each meal. Test the mixtures in small amounts before you start out. If they taste good at home, under optimum conditions, they will taste even better on the trail.

Cooking Equipment Lists

Take along only the equipment you will need for the meals you have planned. For any type of camping trip, the *basic* list of items for six people weighs about 4½ to 5 pounds total, excepting 1 or 2 1-burner stoves (gasoline, alcohol, or butane). The second stove is not an absolute necessity except for winter camping but it is practical and adds convenience. Total weight of cooking equipment of 1 pound per person is not excessive. Take along additional *useful items* as you need them for the group's convenience. If you have less stringent weight and space limitations than do backpackers, fliers, or canoe travelers, you might use both lists — basic items and useful items.

Basic Items:

A set of straight-sided aluminum pots with bail-handles which nest one within the other, with either frying pan covers or flat lids:

     1 one-gallon pot
     1 two- to three-quart pot
     1 one-quart pot
     1 one-pint pot (optional)

1 lightweight wire grill (8 by 12 inches), preferably with folding legs
1 one-gallon plastic water container
1 one-quart plastic shaker (for mixing milk, juice, etc.)
1 metal pancake turner with slotted blade
2 wooden spoons (1 long-handled)
2 paring knives or pocket knives
1 pair pliers
1 ten-ounce Sierra Club cup or similar metal cup
1 plastic sheet (9 by 12 feet), preferably with grommets at corners and along edges
1 roll (40 to 50 feet long) of 1/8-inch nylon cord (for rigging a shelter, or making a "bear bag")
1 pair leather-palm or cloth work gloves
Cloth or plastic bags for carrying pots, equipment, fuel container, etc.
Plastic bags for food
1 one-burner stove (gasoline, alcohol, or butane)
Containers of fuel (see pages 180 through 182)

Useful Items:

1 twelve-inch square or comparably-sized rectangular aluminum or magnesium griddle

178

1 reflector oven (overall size is about 11 by 14 inches, and weight is about 2½ pounds)

1 cast-iron Dutch oven with cover (a useful size is about 16 inches in diameter and 8 to 10 inches deep)

2 square metal baking pans (each 10 inches square, 2 inches deep) (for top-of-the-stove cooking, you can use one as a lid for the other)

1 long-handled fork

1 eight-ounce ladle

1 four-ounce ladle

1 rubber spatula with large blade

1 rubber spatula with narrow blade

1 knife with 8- to 10-inch blade

1 knife with 8- to 9-inch serrated blade

1 French knife with 8- or 9-inch blade

1 pair kitchen shears

6 metal skewers

2 short-handled wooden spoons for mixing or serving

1 rectangular plastic dishpan (This may serve as a salad bowl; container for pudding, gelatin salads or cheesecake; or as a serving bar for beverages and condiments. It is light enough to backpack.)

1 twelve-inch wire rack with handles (for cooking steak and chops over flames, or for toasting bread)

1 one-cup plastic measuring cup

6 or 8 aluminum pie plates

1 twelve-inch square piece of masonite (for cutting board, tray for dry foods, etc.)

1 miners' headlight-type flashlight with battery (for working around camp in the dark)

1 gas lantern with extra mantles

Clean-up Equipment:

1 bar laundry soap (naphtha or floating type)

1 one-pint plastic container for soap powder
  (not detergent)
1 metal or hard-plastic sponge
1 brush with 8-inch wooden handle

Stoves, Ovens, and Bags

Stoves are fast, clean, leave no fire scars, and require less work than wood fires built in pits, trenches, or campground fireplaces. Use a stove where wood is scarce, or in any heavily used camping area. Stoves are sometimes necessary for desert camping but always are for snow camping and camping above timberline where there is no wood. In the future they will be needed more at all times of the year, especially in overused parks and wildlands where wood will be short or nonexistent.

There are many types of stoves on the market. Each has advantages and disadvantages. Talk to friends, check with suppliers, examine the different types, and decide which best suits your requirements. Single-burner stoves are small and efficient for backpackers (winter and summer), for fliers, kayak and canoe travelers, and for all others to whom weight and space are critical. They are reasonably priced.

Those who travel by car, raft, rowboat, pack animal, and dog sled, where lightweight equipment is not vital, may prefer 2-burner stoves. These cook efficiently and fold neatly into a rectangular package approximately 1 foot by 2 feet by 6 inches.

Here is a brief summary of instructions for various kinds of cooking equipment.

Gasoline Stoves. Use only white gasoline. Take only the amount of fuel necessary. A 3-man, 2-day trip requires about 1 quart; a 6-man, 6-day trip requires about 3 quarts, if fuel is carefully used. Fuel is conveniently stored for carrying in 1-quart or smaller metal containers, either flat or round, with screw-tops, tied into separate plastic bags. These should be kept out of the sun and away from flames and heat at all times. *Gasoline is explosive.* Always fill the stove *before* starting the meal. Fill only *cold* stoves.

Butane Stoves. The fuel in butane stoves — liquid petroleum gas — is under pressure in a cylinder or "cartridge." Each cylinder burns 3 to 4 hours of cooking time, which is usually enough for a weekend trip for a small group, and is then replaced by a full one. As with other stoves, 2 are faster and more efficient than 1 for groups larger than 2 people.

For those who can afford the extra weight, LPG (liquified petroleum gas) is practical for longer trips such as those by camper and trailer. A practical unit to burn this gas can be built by attaching 2 or 3 old stove-burners by a plastic hose to a pressure-gauge unit that fits on the outlet of a small LPG tank such as the 5-gallon rental type. The burners are placed under pots supported by rocks or under a folding-legged grill. The heat of each burner is controlled by a valve.

Kerosene Stoves. Use only kerosene. The amount of fuel is about the same as that used by gas stoves. The same kind of container should be used, and the same care in packaging and storing. Kerosene does not evaporate as gas does but is more oily and has a more pervasive odor: keep it away from food supplies and clothing. Nor is it explosive — but keep it away from stoves except when filling. Fill only *cold* stoves, before starting the meal.

Alcohol Stoves. Alcohol is nonexplosive and nontoxic but evaporates easily. It is less efficient than the other fuels because it already contains oxygen, and therefore cooks a bit more slowly than gasoline, kerosene or butane. Half a pint will last for about 1¼ hours. Use the same kind of container as for the other fuels. Fill only *cold* stoves. Two stoves are better than one.

Some people think that 1 or 2 large cans of *sterno* (canned heat) is the best fuel in wet rainy weather. Other people, especially "camper" campers, like the *hibachi* — the Japanese cast iron charcoal brazier. Hibachis vary in size but most measure 1 foot high by 1 foot in diameter; thus they are easily stored, and readily used. A handful or two of charcoal is enough to broil meat for 2 people.

Windscreens. All stoves require windscreens or other protection (a rock or log may do) to operate efficiently. Windscreens usually are made of either folding- or rolled-sheets of aluminum about the height of the stove. Set up the screen around the stove or along its windward side to protect the flame from the wind. Rolled-sheets can be carried wrapped around the pots in the pot sack, or around the stove in the stove sack. Folding-screens will fit into a pack with other flat equipment. One kind or the other is a necessity.

Reflector Ovens. The reflector oven resembles 2 rectangular aluminum "book covers" with 1 "page" between them. When opened, the page becomes the shelf. The covers are propped open at 45°-angles by wires which fit into slots at the end of the shelf. The oven is held upright, about shelf level, by 2 wire frames attached to the outside of the covers. Some models have small sides which fold out on each side of the shelf. The inside of the covers and shelf are highly polished to reflect enough heat to bake whatever item is set on the shelf.

To bake: Set the oven in front of a small fire (more coals than flame) so that the angled polished wings of the oven reflect the heat. Place item(s) to be baked in a lightly greased pan (about 2 inches deep and 9 or 10 inches square) and place pan on center baking shelf.

Dutch Ovens. Camp stews can be cooked in a Dutch oven by setting it on top of a fire or by burying it in coals. You can use it to bake breads, casseroles, or desserts, or to roast meat.

To bake or roast: Lightly grease sides and bottom of oven. Place items to be baked or roasted on bottom of oven. (Before baking, brush biscuits or muffins on both sides with melted butter or oil to aid browning.) Cover oven tightly. Set it in deep coals, and spread more coals over top.

As with all cast-iron utensils, a Dutch oven should be rubbed lightly with cooking oil after washing in order to prevent rusting.

Plastic Bag Cooking. You can heat food successfully by putting it in a plastic bag, placing the closed bag in a pot of water, bringing the water to a boil, and letting it simmer for 10 or 15 minutes. This heating method also works for unopened cans.

Meat should *not be roasted* in plastic bags. The bags explode in the oven, bag particles adhere to the meat, and the result is an essence of plastic. For braised or stewed meat, it is best to remove the meat from its plastic bag, and cook (adding liquid) in covered metal containers.

Building a Fire

If you are camping where no fireplace exists, and have no stove, build a minimal fire pit. Choose a sandy campsite or hard surface wherever possible. But never a meadow, grassy forest site, lake or river bank, or trail.

Clear an area several feet in diameter of leaves and

duff, down to mineral soil. In the center dig a shallow depression 15 to 18 inches long, 8 inches wide, and about 4 inches deep. Save the dirt. Three or 4 small rocks on each side of the trench are enough to support a grill. Build no large stone edifice! If you have a grill with folding legs, you won't need any rocks. Alternatively, it is possible to mound sand or dirt on each side of the trench and rest the grill on that.

Use downed wood sparingly, and *don't cut new wood*. Standing dead tree trunks provide nesting sites for woodpeckers and other birds that help control insect populations and keep the forest healthy.

Lean several 2- or 3-inch sticks or twigs together in a teepee, with a bit of paper, bark, or dry grass, and light them in the center with a match. Add a few larger sticks, being careful not to smother the fire. When it is burning well, lay several sticks, 1 or 2 inches in diameter, the length of the trench. You should now be able to cook over the fire. Feed it steadily but sparingly during the cooking period, and never leave it unattended.

Build only 1 fire; that is, let your cooking fire become your evening campfire. And keep that small. Put it out at night. In case of rain, wrap some wood in a plastic sheet, or stack it under an overhanging rock. Then you will be sure to have dry wood when you rebuild the fire the following morning.

Washing Dishes

Dishwashing should be kept as simple as possible.

Wash dishes in the soup or main dish pot. As soon as a cooking pot is emptied, clean out all food remnants (if not in garbage-can country, you should scatter scrapings widely in the brush or at least away from the camping area or lake or stream) and start heating water in it, with some soap powder or shavings from a bar of soap. Never use detergent.

Let each person wash his own eating utensils. Cups and spoons can be easily cleaned first with sand or dirt, and later rinsed in boiling water.

Pots, too, can be cleaned out first with sand. Never wash them in a stream or lake, or dispose of food or soapy water in any body of water. Wash and rinse pots with boiling water. Don't bother to scrub off the black from the outside; it is beneficial, helping to absorb heat in cooking. Careful scrubbing can be done at home at the end of the trip.

Then either fill the pots with water, cover, and set in a safe place for the next meal; or let them drain overnight on a rock or plastic sheet with the other utensils.

Storing Food

If you are camping in bear country, never hide food in your sleeping bag or pack, day or night. Actually, it is not wise to do this anywhere because the food can attract rodents, and your equipment might be badly damaged or even demolished.

Make a "bear bag" for food storage during the night and whenever you are away from camp. Sack all uncanned foods in a bag about the size of a pillow case. (It should hold about 40 pounds.) Tie the bag to 1 end of a 1/8-inch-diameter nylon rope; tie a small rock to the other end. Throw the rock over a large tree limb, several feet out from the trunk and at least 15 feet above the ground. Pull the bag up so it hangs 2 or 3 feet below the branch, and tie the other end of the rope (now minus rock) to a nearby tree trunk or branch.

An alternative to the bear bag is to wrap the food in a plastic sheet, and leave the bundle with a selection of pots, lids, and utensils placed on top of it. Any intruder will probably be frightened away by the sudden racket of falling pots. If not, the noise will at least alert the campers, who can then chase the bear away by shouting and blinking their flashlights.

Another animal that is expert at getting into food stores is the raccoon. To be raccoon-proof, a cache of food left for any length of time should be packed in a 5-gallon tin with a tight-fitting, recessed lid. And the tin should be hidden well. The latter is a safety precaution against all animals, including the 2-legged kind.

Breaking Camp

Before leaving a wilderness campsite, scatter all waste food (there shouldn't be much if you planned well) for the local wildlife. If they don't eat it, it will dry out and return to the soil.

All burnables should be completely reduced to ashes. All cans should be burned and flattened, and then sacked and packed out along with all bottles and foil. Orange peels can be burned if your fire is very hot. Otherwise you should pack them out, also.

Use enough dirt or water to put out every coal and spark in the fire until you can feel the fire pit with your hands. Then break up the ashes and cold charcoal into fine bits, mix them well with dirt, and scatter over a wide area. Fill the depression in the ground with the sand or dirt you removed when you prepared the fireplace. Restore duff and leaves to the entire area you scraped clean.

In short, do your best to eradicate the site of the fire. Scattered charcoal should be the only evidence remaining.

The Camping Ethic

The places where you camp — both in the wild and at public facilities — will remain attractive, unspoiled and usable only if each camper observes some basic rules. The following nine constitute a good camping ethic.

1. Leave your transistor radio at home. Sound carries far in the out-of-doors, especially in canyon country. Learn to appreciate instead the sounds of birds and animals, and the silence.

2. Leave all firearms at home. No trail or campground is an appropriate place for target practice.

3. When setting up or breaking camp, especially late at night or early in the morning, do be quiet. Keep down the bright lights so any other campers will be disturbed as little as possible. Operate any motorized equipment as quietly as you can, and no longer than absolutely necessary.

4. Keep your camp site tidy. Don't spread clothing, equipment, food containers or packing material on the trail or anywhere it might bother other campers.

5. Do not pound nails into trees for hanging clothes or attaching shelves. This practice damages the trees and disfigures the area.

6. Obey established rules for sanitation and garbage disposal. Put nothing in the lake or stream.

7. Pick up any litter left by previous campers, and drop none yourself. Leaving a campsite clean will encourage those who follow to do the same.

8. When breaking camp, make sure your fire is out.

9. Do not leave behind opened packages of food in shelters or cabins. Your gesture will only attract rodents and render the food unfit for human consumption. Labeled, unopened cans, however, may be left behind in cabins and greatly appreciated eventually by some hungry camper.

Some suppliers of lightweight food

We offer here for your trip preparations a list of some suppliers and sellers of freeze-dried and dehydrated food. If none of these is located in your area, try the local supermarket — many of which have begun to stock lightweight food — or the nearest gourmet shop or health food store.

Ace Sporting Goods Co., 5300 W. 44, Denver, Colorado

Alpine Supply, Laconia, New Hampshire 03246

Alpine Recreation, 455 Central Park Avenue, Scarsdale, New York 01583

Antelope Camping and Equipment Co., 10268 Imperial Avenue, Cupertino, California 95014

L.L. Bean, Freeport, Maine 04032

Camp and Trail, 21 Park Place, New York, New York 10007

Chuck Wagon Foods, Box 226, Woburn, Massachusetts 01801

Cloud Cap Chalet, 625 Southwest 12, Portland, Oregon

Desert-Mountain Sports, 4506 North 16th Street, Phoenix, Arizona 85016

Don Gleason's Campers Supply, Inc., 12 Pearl Street, Northampton, Massachusetts 01060

Dri-Lite Foods, 11333 South Atlantic, Lynwood, California 90264

Eastern Mountain Sports, Inc.
  1041 Commonwealth Avenue, Boston, Massachusetts 02215

Route 9, Amherst, Massachusetts 01002

Main Street, North Conway, New Hampshire 03860

Family Market, 1301 I Street, Anchorage, Alaska 99501

Gary King Sporting Goods, 1231 West Northern Lights Boulevard, Anchorage, Alaska 99501

Gerry, 5450 North Valley Highway, Denver, Colorado 80216

S. Gumpert Co., Inc.
812 Jersey Avenue, Jersey City, New Jersey 07302
425 E. Illinois Street, Chicago, Illinois 60611
3915 Capitol Avenue, Houston, Texas 77023

H & H Surplus & Camper's Haven, 305 W. Baltimore Street, Baltimore, Maryland 21201

Hanson's, 395 South Main Street, Brewer, Maine 04412

Hickory Farms of Ohio, Western Division, 1374 Saticoy Street, Van Nuys, California (also Mill Valley, San Anselmo, Palo Alto, and San Jose, California; and Honolulu, Hawaii)

Holubar Mountaineering Ltd., 1975 30th Street, Boulder, Colorado 80302

Kelty, 1801 Victory Boulevard, Glendale, California 91201

Leon Greenman, 132 Spring Street, New York, New York 10012

Moor & Mountain, 67 Main Street, Concord, Massachusetts 01742

Mountain House, 1028 Sir Francis Drake Boulevard, Kentfield, California 94904

The Mountain Shop, 228 Grant Avenue, San Francisco, California 94108

The Mountain Shop, 189 Linden Street, Wellesley, Massachusetts 02181

The North Face, 1234 5th Street, Berkeley, California 94710

Oregon Freeze-Dry Foods Inc., Albany, Oregon 97321

Perma Pak, 40 East 2430 So., Salt Lake City, Utah

Recreational Equipment, Inc., 1525 11th Avenue, Seattle, Washington 98122

Rich-Moor Lite Weight Camp Foods, P.O. Box 2728, Van Nuys, California 91404

The Ski Hut, 1615 University Avenue, Berkeley, California 94703

Skimeister Ski Shop, Main Street, North Woodstock, New Hampshire 03262

The Smilie Company, 575 Howard Street, San Francisco, California 94105

The Sports Chalet, 906 W. Northern Lights Boulevard, Anchorage, Alaska 99501

Stod Nichols, Inc., Theatre Building, Littleton, New Hampshire 03561

Stow-a-way Sports Industries, Inc., 166 Cushing Highway, Cohasset, Massachusetts 02025

Surplus City, 1113 East 2nd, Roswell, New Mexico 88201

Thomas Black & Sons, 930AP Ford Street, Ogdensburg, New York 03669

Thompson Foods
4706 North 7th Avenue, Phoenix, Arizona 85013
120 South Mesa Drive, Mesa, Arizona 85204

Totem Pole, Route 114, North Andover, Massachusetts 01845

Trail Chef, 2140 51st, Los Angeles, California 90015

Veteran's Sport Shop, 281 Asylum Street, Hartford, Connecticut 06103

Wick's Ski Shops
1201 Philadelphia Pike, Wilmington, Delaware
321 West Woodland Avenue, Springfield, Pennsylvania 19064

Index of recipes

Alfalfa Sprouts for Salad,
  139
Apple Pancakes, 151
Apple Pie, 165
Apricot Pie, 167
Argentine Roast Beef Ribs,
  42
Avocado Pineapple Salad,
  126
Avocado Salad, 126
Baked Ham with Guava
  and Sherry, 73
Baked Lima Beans, 117
Bean Salad, 127
Beans and Ham, 71
Beans, Paul's Way, 116
Beans with Cheese, 115
Beef and Oyster Pie 45
Beef or Lamb Curry
  (Cream Style), 52
Beer Tartare, 40
Beef with Mushrooms, 47
Beet Salad, 125
Beets and Greens, 120
Black-Eyed Peas, 75
Brains and Eggs, 105
Broiled Salmon Steaks, 94

Buckwheat Groats
  (for Breakfast), 25
Buckwheat Groats
  (for Dinner), 114
Buttermilk Biscuits, 144
Cabbage and Raisin Salad,
  133
Cabbage, Apples, and
  Cranberries, 121
Cabbage with Sour
  Cream, 129
Camp Baked Apples, 159
Camp Coffee, 169
Camper's Chutney, 154
Camper's Roux, 154
Caper Mayonnaise for
  Poached Salmon, 157
Cappuccino, 171
Carob Drink, 171
Carrot and Raisin Salad, 133
Cheese Omelet, 108
Chicken and Dumplings, 85
Chicken and Rice, 82
Chicken and Rice,
  Trail Version, 83
Chicken Gumbo, 86
Chinese Cabbage Salad, 129

Chocolate Frosting, 160
Coffee Cream Sauce, 165
Coffee Pudding, 161
Cole Slaw, 130
Cooked Salad Dressing, 157
Corned Beef and Cabbage, 43
Cornish Pasties, 59
Corn Pone Bread, 147
Cousin Jack Pasty, 60
Creamed Tuna with Ginger over Noodles, 99
Cucumber Salad, 134
Cucumbers, Radishes, and Onions, 134
Curried Fish Steaks, 96
Curried Rice and Potatoes, 114
Dandelion Greens, 123
Dessert Fruit Salad, 159
Deviled Cabbage and Cucumber Salad, 132
Deviled Eggs, Curried, 108
Dried Apples, 25
Dumplings, 148
Eggplant Salad, 135
Enchiladas, 57
English Fruit Cake, 166
Familia, 27
Fish Baked in the Coals, 90
Flat Bread, 143
Flemish Beef Stew, 44
Fresh Peach Sauce, 156

Fried Catfish, 91
Fried Chicken and Gravy, 84
Fried Rabbit with Gravy, 88
Fruit Compote for Pancakes, 155
Fruit Salad, 136
Garlic Sausage and Sauerkraut, 77
Ginger Fish, 97
Glazed Carrots, 120
Glazed Carrots and Apples, 121
Golden (Bob) Trout Parmesan, 93
Golden Corn Bread, 145
Golden Rice, 112
Golden Risotto, 76
Granola, 26
Grapefruit and Onion Salad, 132
Green Beans, Almonds, and Bacon, 119
Green Salad with Peas, 136
Green Salad, Italian, 137
Guacamole, 125
Ham and Oyster Pie, 74
Ham Biscuits or Ham Corn Bread, 143
Hamburger and Potato Cakes, 53
Ham Slices, 73

Hash, 49
Headhunter Fried Rice, 101
Headhunter Fried Rice,
    Trail Style, 102
Hekka, 50
Herbed Celery Root, 122
Hot Slaw, 131
Huevos Rancheros, 106
Hunter's Stew I, 66
Hunter's Stew II, 67
Instant Breakfast, 24
Instant Creamy Potatoes,
    111
Instant Potato Salad, 138
Irish Stew, 69
Jerky, 28
Kidney Bean Salad, 128
Korean Beef and
    Mushrooms, 51
Lamarou, 100
Leek and Potato Soup, 35
Letters from Home, 58
Liver Pâté, 79
Mahimahi Steaks, 98
Marinades, 38
Maryland Scrapple, 78
Meat Ball Pancakes, 54
Meats and Other Treats for
    the Skewer and Open
    Fire, 37
Medium Cream Sauce, 152
Mexican Chocolate, 170
Mincemeat, 48

Minestrone, 36
Mocha, 171
Molasses Chocolate Cooky
    Squares, 164
Molded Salmon Salad, 140
Mountain Lemonade, 173
Mountain Mint Julep, 173
Mushroom Omelet, 107
Mushroom Sauce, 153
Müsli, 29
New England Baked Beans,
    118
Paella, Trail Version, 81
Paella Valenciana, 80
Pan Grilled Steak, 41
Papaya, Avocado and
    Grapefruit Salad, 127
Peach Cobbler, 163
Peas and Cheese Salad, 142
Peppermint Tea, 172
Pie Pastry, 160
Pimento Cheese Spread,
    109
Pineapple Upside-Down
    Cake, 162
Poppyseed Drop Biscuits,
    146
Potato Soup, 34
Potatoes with Cheese,
    110
Pound Cake and Fruit, 161
Quick Trail Breakfast, 25
Rabbit Borracho, 89

Red and Green Cabbage, 131
Rice for Ducks and Other Fowl, 113
Salmon Gumbo, 95
Salsa Caliente (Hot Sauce), 153
Sand Tarts, 162
Sausage Omelet, 107
Sautéed Bananas, 158
Scrambled Eggs with Basil, 103
Scrambled Eggs with Chorizo, 104
Scrambled Eggs with Herbs, 104
Scrambled Eggs with Tomatoes, 105
Shallow-Fried Sweet Potatoes, 110
Shortbread, 164
Short Ribs Western, 43
Shrimp Salad, 141
Shrimp Salad Dressing, 156
Soesatie, 70
Sonofabitch Stew, 46
Sour Cream Slaw, 130
Sourdough Pancakes, 150
Sourdough Pancakes with Blueberries, 150
Sourdough Starter for Pancakes, 149
Spaghetti and Beef Sauce, 61

Spicy Lamb Stew, 68
Spinach in Cream, 122
Stewed Sweet Potatoes, 112
Sweet-and-Sour Pork Steaks, 72
Tamale Pie, 56
Tea, 170
Texas Chili con Carne, 55
Thin Cream Sauce, 152
Tomato Aspic, 140
Trail Stew, 41
Tripe and Dumplings, 62
Tripe and Onion Stew, 63
Tuna Chowder, 98
Tuna Salad, 141
Turnips and Greens, 123
Vegetable Salad, 142
Vegetable Sauce, 155
Vegetable Soup, 33
Vegetables Roasted in Coals, 124
Venison Hawaiian, 64
Venison Steaks, 64
Venison Stew, 65
Whipped Sweet Potatoes, 111
White Bean Salad, 128
Wild Duck Roast, 87
Wild Rose Hip Soup, 168
Wilted Lettuce Salad, 135
Wine-marinated Steak or Shish Kebabs, 71